LABYRINTH

A Historical Guide to Why American Medical Bills Became So Complicated and How They Can Get Better

TIMOTHY J. GARRETT, M.D.

ISBN: 979-8-9992039-0-8

DEDICATED TO MORT SALOMON, M.D.

FOR TAKING A CHANCE ON ME, TEACHING ME, AND BEING MY FRIEND.

TABLE OF CONTENTS

PREFACE

It is late 1964, and the young mother-to-be is alone. Her husband of just over a year has shipped out to South Korea with his Army unit, and she has moved from their little apartment near Fort Ord, California, back home to the hills of northern Georgia.

Pretty soon, she feels the contractions that signal that her little one is on the way. She goes to the hospital and is promptly admitted to the labor ward. She knows the hospital well because this is where she completed her nursing training just the year before. Well-wishers form a steady stream by her room as her labor pains become more frequent.

At 2:30 in the morning, she gives birth to a healthy baby boy. As the Red Cross begins its attempts to contact the soldier in South Korea to tell him he has a son, the staff of the hospital cares for the new mother and baby. The two will be in the hospital for 5 days.

On the day they are being discharged, the mother is presented with a slip of paper. It is the hospital bill – a form, custom-printed for the hospital and filled out by hand – and it itemizes the various services and supplies. It is a short list – 5 days of room-and-board, some delivery room supplies, and a few medicines. The total charge - $105. The new mother pays the amount out of the savings that the young couple have put aside over the past year for this very purpose.

As we sit in the 21st century and look back at this quaint scene, it is hard to imagine. Americans are now accustomed to excruciatingly complex medical bills, with charges that only the very wealthiest can afford to cover out-of-pocket.

It came as no surprise when, in 2022, a survey appeared claiming that almost 40% of Americans said their medical bills were somewhat or extremely confusing.[1] Actually, it *is* surprising that the percentage was not much higher. It has become cliché to talk about the myriad charges on medical bills. My friends use characterizations like "Greek" and "chicken scratch" to describe the language on healthcare claims.

[1] Richard Payerchin, "Medical bills cause confusion for almost 40% of patients," *Medical Economics*, December 19, 2022, accessed April 29, 2025, https://www.medicaleconomics.com/view/medical-bills-cause-confusion-for-almost-40-of-patients

However, it is not just an issue on which to base jokes. These complicated bills can hide errors – including reporting incorrect procedures or even services that were not provided at all.

This is a particularly important problem for older Americans. In 2023, the *Consumer Financial Protection Bureau* (CFPB) reported that providers are billing millions of Americans who have Medicare and Medicaid coverage for amounts they do not owe. The CFPB blames this largely on medical bills that are difficult or impossible to understand.[2]

Confusing bills have real world effects. A Consumer Reports survey conducted in 2018 showed that more than a third of respondents paid bills they were not sure they owed, including 20% of that group paying more than $1,000.[3]

The young couple mentioned at the beginning of this preface were my parents, and I was the baby that generated such a reasonable hospital bill. In the decades that followed that week in November 1964 – while the complexity of American medical bills was exponentially expanding – I grew up, earned a medical degree, had a career as an emergency room (ER) doctor, and went to business school. Over the past decade and a half, I have been a physician executive and have worked in companies that assist doctors, hospitals, and insurance companies in managing the maze of forms and portals, rules and regulations, and all the other things that complicate the process of paying and getting paid for healthcare services.

My goal in this book is not to be an apologist for the current state of medical bills. Instead, this book is intended to explore how we got to this level of complexity in the United States, explain current medical bills so that you may understand them better, and discuss what we can do to improve the way we as a nation handle medical claims.

Even though I will be careful to explain the evolution and current state of medical bills as clearly as possible, it may still be confusing to you. Therefore, each chapter will end with a section I call "Breadcrumbs for the Labyrinth." Like Hansel and Gretel[4] before you and brave Theseus who uncoiled string to escape the

---

[2] "Medical Billing and Collections Among Older Americans," Consumer Financial Protection Bureau website, last modified Sep. 18, 2024, accessed April 29, 2025, https://www.consumerfinance.gov/data-research/research-reports/issue-spotlight-medical-billing-and-collections-among-older-americans

[3] "Sick of Confusing Medical Bills?" Consumer Reports website, last modified August 1, 2018, accessed April 29, 2025, https://www.consumerreports.org/medical-billing/sick-of-confusing-medical-bills/

[4] Christine Goldberg, "Hansel and Gretel," *The Greenwood Encyclopedia of Folktales and Fairy Tales* (2008)

original labyrinth[5], I trust you will find these summaries at the end of each chapter helpful to keep track of the twists and turns you encounter.

By the end, I hope that we will all have a better awareness of the challenges facing everyone involved in this environment that we call the American healthcare system. This includes providers (hospitals, doctors, and other clinicians), payers (insurance companies, health plans, and employers), and individuals (you and me).

Now, let's venture into the Labyrinth.

[5] The Myth of Theseus and the Minotaur, Greek Myths and Greek Mythology website, accessed June 20, 2025, https://www.greekmyths-greekmythology.com/myth-of-theseus-and-minotaur.

CHAPTER 1

A LONG LOOK BACK

Thomas de Burgh is sick. Very sick.

He is sitting in his bed chamber, hands on his knees, trying to catch his breath. He woke in the middle of the night after a tortuous dream and found that his wind had left him again.

Nay, not again, he thinks.

The same thing had happened several months ago on his last visit to London, and Thomas had suffered through a handful of other occurrences. On those occasions, as now, his manservant had summoned the physician.

This particular physician is well known to the family. Trained in the world-renowned Italian medical school in Bologna, he has been treating Thomas's father and brothers and their families for years.

The physician quickly examines Thomas, inspects the urine specimen by the chair, and prepares for treatment. He chats with Thomas about the recent coronation of King Henry in the abbey at Westminster and how the physician has recently attended to Thomas's older brother, as much to brag about his proximity to power as to calm his patient's nerves.

The lancet is sharp and almost painlessly slices into the vein on Thomas's arm. The physician carefully observes the flow of blood into the chamber pot he has placed on the floor at Thomas's side. He plans to let a substantial amount this time, hoping to quickly ease his patron's symptoms and to hopefully delay any future recurrence. When Thomas swoons slightly, the physician places a compress over the incision and wraps a bandage around the arm.

The physician helps Thomas back to bed, prescribes a small glass of wine but no water or meat, and leaves the house.

By later in the day, Thomas feels much better – well enough to go to a banquet hosted by his brother. He thinks, A little meat surely would not harm.

The physician is paid a large annual sum for the expertise he uses in the service of the family – though gentlemen do not publicly discuss such things, and thus arrangements are made in private moments.[6]

---

[6] Thomas de Burgh was a real person and was constable of Norwich in the reigns of Kings John and Henry III. His older brother was magnate of Henry III beginning when the king was only 12 years old. There is no recorded evidence that Thomas suffered from congestive heart failure, as the fictitious account above suggests.

You may wonder why a story about a patient and physician from 1220 – just after the second coronation of English King Henry III – has anything to do with 21st century American medical bills.

The underpinnings of modern medical coding and billing are as old as medicine itself and bring in such factors and philosophies as the physician-patient relationship, medicine's responsibility for care of the poor, and the expectation of individual physicians to provide emergency care when necessary. It is therefore instructive to see how medical care was provided and how payment was made for medical services in prior centuries as a way of understanding the intent of current reimbursement systems. We will therefore spend this chapter looking back in time to eras very different from ours.

Medicine Before Medical Bills

The medicine practiced in medieval times – that is the Middle Ages or Dark Ages, roughly 450 A.D. through 1450 – was greatly influenced by Galen and other Greek and Roman medical practitioners from antiquity. Galen proposed the theory that four main "humors" determined the health of human beings. When these humors were out of balance, disease could occur. The treatment of disease was therefore focused on reestablishing the balance of humors.

In Thomas de Burgh's example, his physician apparently considered that his "sanguine humor" had become too predominant, causing him to appear hot and moist. Therefore, bloodletting was a direct attempt at decreasing this unbalanced humor.

In today's age, Thomas would have been diagnosed as having an acute exacerbation of chronic congestive heart failure. Fortunately for Thomas, the proper modern treatment of acute heart failure involves, in part, the removal of fluid from the blood stream with medications called diuretics. Thus, blood-letting serves some of the same purpose.

Though 21st century medical technology has passed far beyond bloodletting, payment for medical care in our century shares some similarities and many important differences from medieval physician remuneration.

Payment by Status and Obligation

Healthcare in the Middle Ages was provided in what can only be called a multi-tiered system. Those in the upper socioeconomic strata like Thomas de Burgh – whether wealthy merchants, nobility, or royalty – could have access to professionals who had actual medical training. These doctors of medicine received a broad education in Greek, Latin, the humanities, Galen's theories of the four humors, and –

if in a time and place in which religious authorities allowed dissection of human bodies – human anatomy.

Educated physicians practicing in England could not legally bill their patients or sue them if they failed to pay. They were required to follow the Roman practice that had come down through the ages of instead accepting an "honorarium" that were presumably voluntary. This rule around payments applied only to physicians, and not to barber-surgeons that we will meet later in this chapter.[7]

Despite the inability to directly bill their patients, trained and learned physicians who confined their practices to higher classes commanded an income incomprehensible to practitioners of more lowly positions. Dr. Erin Connelly, professor in the School of Life Sciences at the University of Warwick and an expert on medieval medicine, states that medical and surgical treatises from the late medieval period point to a structure in which payment for services was based on the patient's social and financial status. Thus, wealthy patients often paid extravagant sums by the standards of the day, while patients who were very poor many times were not expected to pay anything.[8]

This altruistic approach toward the poor stemmed from at least a couple of sources. First, the ancient Greek and Roman philosophical pillars of medicine included an obligation to treat the poor. Though accounts of the greediness of Greek and Roman physicians seem to be more numerous than descriptions of generosity, it is clear that many ancient physicians provided care at greatly reduced rates for people of lesser means and often charged no fee at all.[9]

Second, before the thirteenth century, the practice of medicine in western Europe was largely confined to monks and other members of the clergy. Application of the healing arts was felt to be a natural outgrowth of Christ's command to serve the poor.[10]

Even after the profession of medicine spread beyond the sole duty of the Church, the commitment to make provision for those who could not afford treatment permeated the profession. This commitment has survived to modern times and is reflected in charity expectations in nonprofit hospitals, laws that stipulate a duty to treat, and many healthcare practitioners' own personal obligations to offer care to those who cannot afford it.

---

[7] Mark Hall, et al, Learning from the Legal History of Billing for Medical Fees, *Journal of General Internal Medicine* (2008) 23(8):1257–60

[8] Personal correspondence with Dr. Connolly, May 2025.

[9] Norman Underwood, "Medicine, Money, and Christian Rhetoric: The Socio-Economic Dimensions of Healthcare in Late Antiquity," *Studies in Late Antiquity* (2018) 2 (3): 342–384.

[10] E. A. Hammond, "Incomes of Medieval English Doctors," *Journal of the History of Medicine and Allied Sciences* (1960) 15, no. 2: 154-169

With at least some commitment of medieval physicians to providing free care or treatment at reduced fees to the poor, this meant that income had to be realized where it could be had.

Dr. Connelly points to the writings of medieval French surgeon Henri de Mondeville as a window into the financial arrangements of physicians with their patients in the Middle Ages. Mondeville's writing sets out a sliding scale of fees for patients of different socioeconomic strata. I can state his thoughts no more clearly than Henri can himself, and so here is what he wrote:

"The first class are paupers who must be treated for nothing: the second class are a little better off and may send presents of fowls and ducks; they pay in kind.

The third class are friends or relatives who pay no fixed fee, but send victuals or presents in token of gratitude but no money…

Then there is a class embracing those who are notoriously bad payers, such as our nobility and their households, government officials, judges, baillies [court officials], and lawyers whom we are obliged to treat because we dare not offend them. In fact, the longer we treat these people the more we lose. It is best to cure them as quickly as possible and to give them the best medicines.

Lastly there is a class who pay in full, and in advance, and they should be prevented from getting ill at all, because we are paid a salary to keep them in health."[11]

Through Mondeville's words, we can see payment tiers that are not unlike different payment methodologies that we see today.

The first class resembles today's charity care. As an emergency physician in a traditional "county hospital", I was well accustomed with the patient who had no insurance coverage and no job – or possibly a job with very little income. We expected very little money if any from these "self-pay" patients. Those who were able to pay a little might fall into Mondeville's second class – though I never received a duck as payment for ER services.

The third class bears some resemblance to the "professional courtesy" arrangement that used to be a standard practice among physicians, though it has fallen out of favor with more recent state fair-pay statutes. In my career in the ER, I would note on a claim form that a physician colleague's ER visit would not be billed – my medical colleagues in town would do the same for me and my family.

The section dealing with the badly paying class lays out something of a prospective payment system. In other words, the physician is being paid to treat a condition. It is in the physician's best interest to treat the condition as quickly and effectively as possible in order to maximize the money per day that is received. Any delay only

---

[11] Mondeville quoted in "Treatises of fistula in ano, haemorrhoids, and clysters / by John Arderne," In the digital collection *Corpus of Middle English Prose and Verse,* University of Michigan Library Digital Collections, accessed May 11, 2025, https://name.umdl.umich.edu/ArderneFistula.

dilutes the set payment. In later chapters, we will see that this arrangement has some similarities to the current diagnostic related group (DRG) system for inpatient stays and the ambulatory payment classification (APC) system for outpatient services.

The last of Mondeville's classes pays a retainer to the physician. Medieval physicians attending the wealthy in Europe were often paid on a retainer basis, receiving a set annual sum for the ongoing provision of any needed medical services. This appears similar to the *concierge medicine* practices that have sprung up over the past couple of decades in the U.S. One could also make the point that *capitated fees* that became popular in the 1970s and 1980s in the U.S. could be considered similar to the medieval retainer system.

In other accounts, we see evidence of other payment methodologies. One such account is that of Bishop Mitford of Salisbury, who became ill in late 1406. After a series of encounters with local practitioners, the bishop became sick enough to summon from Oxford a more prominent physician, Master Thomas Thirlwall. Despite intensive treatment over a period of a few months, the bishop's health continued to deteriorate. Eventually, Thirlwall called upon his colleague, eminent physician John Malvern, to attend the bishop with him. Both before and after Malvern's participation in the care of the patient, an array of different medications and treatments were employed.

By May, it was clear to the physicians that the bishop would not recover. Malvern returned to Oxford, and Bishop Mitford died a few days later.

The account of the bill (or more accurately, request for an honorarium) reveals that the bishop's estate was charged for the medications, for the physicians' fees, and for travel expenses – including those of Malvern's six servants – though there was no charge for room and board of the entourage. The total amount was 16 pounds, 10 shillings - a princely sum that exceeded the annual income of all but the very wealthiest Englishmen.[12] We see in this account evidence of what would be called in modern times an itemized bill paid in a fee-for-service manner.

Of course, there were no standardized bill forms in medieval England. As we have seen, there is also no evidence of a standard fee schedule or even widespread agreement on what was usual and customary for a physician to charge. The physician based his charges on what was felt the patient should be expected to pay, and this depended on the patient's socioeconomic status. This general practice persisted in Europe and America into the 20th century.

---

[12] Carole Rawcliffe, *Medicine and Society in Later Medieval England*, (1995) pp.104-105 – quoting *Household Accounts from Medieval England*, (1992) pp. 261-430.

Healers, Barber-Surgeons, and Hospitals

Though those in lower classes of society had less access to university-trained physicians, there were other practitioners who stepped in to provide less expensive care.

"Wise women", also known as "cunning women" or "pellars", were traditional healers who came from the local community and provided medical treatment and assistance with childbirth. These practitioners used such methods as bloodletting and herbal remedies to treat various maladies.[13] A network of female healers arose as the wise women passed on their knowledge of herbal medicine and labor and delivery to their daughters and granddaughters.[14] Not only were wise women more plentiful than trained physicians and thus more accessible, they were also much less expensive. An interesting sidenote is that my own great-grandmother, a descendant of English immigrants living in the Blue Ridge mountains of Georgia, was known as a "conjurer" – a traditional healer in the same vein as the wise women of England.

Another important non-physician healthcare practitioner in the Middle Ages was the barber-surgeon. These professionals, when not cutting hair and shaving, used their blades and knowledge of the human body to perform minor surgical procedures.

The English guild of barbers – the Worshipful Company of Barbers – oversaw the quality, work, and training of barber-surgeons in medieval England. This guild was formed at least as early as the twelfth century, initially as a religious and trade organization with a pronounced social bent. As the years went by, the guild evolved into a professional society, with much attention given to the initial training of barber-surgeons and the continuing education of its professional members.[15]

In 1882, a member of the Barbers' Guild, Sidney Young, requested permission to search the records of the guild in Guildhall, London. He spent the next eight years organizing records that stretched back over more than 500 years to Richard le Barber, the first Master of the Barbers' Guild. Mr. Young not only produced a chronological account of the ancient guild, he also reproduced from handwritten parchments and other similar documents ledgers that give a glimpse into the medieval practice of surgery.

The annals of the guild reveal that medieval barber-surgeons initially assisted monks in the medical treatment of persons under their care by performing

---

[13] "Medieval Manuscripts blog," British Library website https://blogs.bl.uk/digitisedmanuscripts/2024/10/index.html. October 31, 2024; accessed May 29, 2025.

[14] "Herbal Medicine in the Middle Ages," Medieval History website. Last modified January 13, 2023, accessed May 29, 2025, https://historymedieval.com/herbal-medicine-in-the-middle-ages

[15] Sidney Young, *The Annals of the Barber-Surgeons of London (*1890), Appearing in the Project Gutenberg eBook. https://www.gutenberg.org/files/49011/49011-0.txt

bloodletting, extraction of teeth, cauterization, the draining of abscesses, and other minor operations. At the 1163 Council of Tours, Pope Alexander III decreed that the shedding of blood was inappropriate for members of the clergy and that monks and priests were forbidden from performing surgery. The clergy thus shifted its focus to the medical care of the sick and turned over the practice of surgery to the barber-surgeons, who by this point were well-prepared to practice independently.

Though there is no "fee schedule" in the Barber annals, there are some glimpses into expenses related to the practice of surgery. A prominent expense seen in many accounts was payments for bodies to be dissected and associated expenses. These autopsies, mostly referred to as "Anatomies" in the Annals, were public affairs and were held in the guild's own anatomy theater, formerly located in the area near the Barbican Center in present-day London. One account lists the expenses for all autopsies performed in the year 1646, with the total coming to 17 pounds, 13 shillings, 6 pence (just over $4,000 in 21st century terms).

There are also mentions of expenses offered toward the well-being of members of the Guild who served as ship's surgeons in the Royal Navy (a lot who were famously underpaid) and fines that were levied on barber-surgeons. These fines were mostly related to missing required autopsies and other training sessions, though other offenses include keeping one's shop open on the Sabbath, speaking out of turn during an official meeting, and practicing medicine (instead of confining one's work to the surgical arts).[16]

Turning our attention from practitioner services to hospital care, we find that there was also a clear difference between the classes in utilization of hospitals. The medieval English hospital mostly aided only the poor. Wealthy persons, in addition to being attended to by trained physicians, expected to be cared for in the comfort of their own homes.[17]

In the Middle Ages, the term "hospital" was applied to four main types of entities: leper facilities, almshouses, shelters for poor travelers and religious pilgrims, and institutions that cared for poor people with some illness – usually a chronic illness.

Leper houses were intended to isolate the occupants from the public more than to offer specific care. The ones in England were mostly founded between the late 11th and early 13th century and were largely in decline by the mid-fifteenth century.

Almshouses offered a place of living for those who were too poor to support themselves. No medical or nursing care was provided in either almshouses or hospices for poor travelers and pilgrims – that is, unless the person fell acutely ill during their stay at which point the laypersons within the facility would offer help.

---

[16] Sidney Young, *The Annals of the Barber-Surgeons of London.*

[17] Carole Rawcliffe, *Medicine and Society in Later Medieval England*, p.205

The least common type of hospital in medieval England was the establishment that cared for the sick poor. It is estimated that of the over 1,100 English hospitals in the Middle Ages, only twenty were devoted solely to the non-leprous sick.[18]

A prominent example of these hospitals for the sick is St. Bartholomew's Hospital in Smithfield, London. St. Bartholomew's was first established in 1123. It is considered the oldest hospital in the world that is still functioning in its original location. From the beginning, St. Bart's offered medical and nursing care for London residents. It was so beloved that, when Henry VIII dissolved all Catholic monasteries as part of the Reformation and the hospital was at risk of closure due to loss of its funding, the citizens of London petitioned the crown to keep St. Bart's open. Henry VIII relented and granted the hospital to the city of London.[19]

I have had the honor of visiting St. Bart's. Only one portion of the medieval building still stands – the tower of the hospital chapel. I learned just before my visit that my ancestor, Sir William Garrard (Garrett), was a key supporter of the hospital in the 16th century.[20] Though much has changed since my forebear served the hospital, St. Bartholomew's still stands as a haven of care for its patients. Walking through its open bays of beds separated by curtains, it was as if I had been transported back in time, if not to the Middle Ages, at least to a time when great legends of science, medicine, and nursing roamed these same halls. (In the world of fiction, Arthur Conan Doyle's Sherlock Holmes and Dr. Watson first met in the laboratory of St. Bartholomew's.)

St. Bartholomew's Hospital was not the only constant presence as the years of the Middle Ages scrolled by. The network of physicians, clergy-based caregivers, wise women, and hospitals for the poor remained essentially unchanged through the mid 15th century.

From Observation to Classification

However, things began to change around 1450. Constantinople fell to the Turks and thus ended the last remnants of the Roman empire. At the same time, the innovations in art and science of the early Romans started to flourish again in Florence and spread across Europe. The Renaissance had begun.

---

18 Martha Carlin, "Medieval English Hospitals', in *The Hospital in History*, ed. Granshaw, L. and Porter, R., (1990) pp. 22-25.

19 "St. Bartholomew's Hospital: Our History," National Health Service website, accessed May 19, 2025, https://www.bartshealth.nhs.uk/st-bartholomews-our-history

20 "Member Biography of Sir William Garrard (Garrett)," The History of Parliament website, accessed May 19, 2025, https://historyofparliamentonline.org/volume/1509-1558/member/garrard

In the field of healthcare, more scientific approaches to medicine and public health took root. The Bills of Mortality – lists of diseases that had caused death in the various corners of London – sprang up in the late 16th century. The weekly publication was one of the first examples in the early modern era of health statistics that helped guide the provision of care or at least inform the public about areas of the city to avoid.[21]

The 19th century saw a steep increase in the use of modern scientific tools to impact medical care. From Florence Nightingale's statistics on infections in the wounded to Lister's antiseptic techniques to Jenner's smallpox vaccine, evidence-based approaches began to revolutionize healthcare.

Despite these scientific advances in the practice of medicine, payment for healthcare remained chained to opaque processes as the turn of the 20th century neared. From the transition of medical practice from the clergy to secular practitioners until then, there had been a business side of medicine. However, payments were inconsistent and were dependent on factors that often were known only to the practitioner. Charges for medical services had the threat of being arbitrary.

At the same time, by the late 1800s, many features had become ingrained in the way people thought about healthcare services as medicine passed from the time of Galen through the Middle Ages and into the modern era. Foremost was that the relationship between the practitioner and the patient was important, even sacred.

Second was that a well-functioning society required that everyone has access to at least some level of medical care. Of course, different levels of care came at different costs, some much higher than others, and the level of care many times depended on the training and expertise of the practitioner.

As the 19th century came to a close, the related idea that all people, regardless of social or economic class, deserved some degree of benefit from the larger society became an increasingly important thought, especially in the American experience. Labor unions, farmers' organizations such as the Grange and the People's Party, and the 1896 nomination of populist William Jennings Bryan as the Democratic candidate for the American presidency were all signs and symptoms of a groundswell of support for the "common man".[22]

However, in the realm of modern medical billing – a field that was essentially nonexistent in 1890 – there was one 19th century development that overshadows everything else, a foundation without which today's medical coding system could not arise. It began with a Frenchman but really took off at an 1893 meeting in Chicago.

---

[21] Niall Boyce, "Bills of Mortality: tracking disease in early modern London," *Lancet*, (2020) 395(10231):1186–1187. https://pmc.ncbi.nlm.nih.gov/articles/PMC7154511/

[22] Charles Postel, "American Populism, 1876-1896," Northern Illinois University Digital Library, accessed May 29, 2025, https://digital.lib.niu.edu/illinois/gildedage/populism

At that meeting, a paper was presented called "Bertillon's report on the nomenclature of diseases, causes of death, and incapacity for work, including hospital admissions," the first large compilation of health information gathered from around the world.[23]

Today, we know it better by a different name – the International Classification of Diseases, or the ICD – and, in time, it would change everything.

[23] Iwao Moriyama, et al, "History of the Statistical Classification of Diseases and Causes of Death," Centers for Disease Control and Prevention website, accessed May 29, 2025, p. 11. https://www.cdc.gov/nchs/data/misc/classification_diseases2011.pdf

Chapter 1: Breadcrumbs for the Labyrinth

- Over hundreds of years, from medieval times through the 19th century, medical care in western Europe and later in America slowly evolved from the province of the clergy to secular healthcare practitioners.
- Payments were highly dependent on the socioeconomic status of the patient and the level of training of the practitioner.
- Throughout this evolution, the physician-patient relationship remained sacred, and it was widely felt that every person deserved access to at least some level of healthcare.
- Charges for healthcare services in medieval times through the 1800s were opaque, based on factors known only to the practitioner, and carried the threat of being arbitrary.
- The scientific and industrial revolution of the 19th century extended to healthcare, with many new tools, techniques, and medications being brought to bear on a wide range of diseases.

CHAPTER 2

THE WORLD REMADE

Errett Graham can hardly believe his eyes.

Over the past few days, he has seen sights that almost no one from his little town of Irvington, Indiana, has seen in their lives. He has walked through gleaming white buildings, bigger than any he has ever imagined, one of them being the largest building in the world at the time. He, his sister Mary, and his mother have ridden Mr. Ferris's wheel that took them to a point higher than the crown of the Statue of Liberty. He has eaten a new kind of sandwich, called a hamburger, and has even seen a two-headed pig.

He is now staring at a sign – *Buffalo Bill Cody and his Wild West Show.*

Buffalo Bill! Errett has read all about him in the serials that Papa brings home from time to time. Now, here is his chance to see the legend in person. He checks his pocket for change – good, there's a quarter!

Errett runs toward the midway. As he passes the Palace of Art, a group of men in business attire walk into his path. The men chat among themselves, large bundles of papers in their hands and held under their arms. Just as Errett has come to expect elsewhere in the exposition grounds, he hears a mixture of languages from the men – German, English, French.

One of the men says in French-tinged English, "Slow down, boy! You do not wish to take out the world's greatest statisticians all at once, do you?" He chuckles.

Errett slows. "Where are all of you going?"

The Frenchman says, "To the Palace of Art. We have an important meeting there."

Errett says, "Well, all right, but it can't be more important than seeing Buffalo Bill! Ain't this place great! So many new things!" Errett continues on his way.

The men smile. The Frenchman says, "New things, indeed."[24]

Counting Disease at the World's Fair

[24] Chicago's Newberry Library offers an online version of Errett McLeod Graham's diary he wrote during his visit to the 1893 Chicago Columbian Exposition. (https://collections.newberry.org/asset-management/2KXJ8Z44DMZ5) Though the report that would become the ICD was presented at a meeting in the Palace of Art on the exposition grounds, there is no evidence that Errett met the report's authors.

Serving as a celebration of the 400th anniversary of Columbus's landing in the Americas, Chicago's 1893 Columbian Exposition brought many innovations to the public including Cracker Jack, the Ferris Wheel, and brownies, and it was at the Exposition that the Pabst beer company won its blue ribbon.[25]

However, the innovation that would arguably have the most widespread effect was introduced in the meetings of the International Statistical Society (ISS), held in the Palace of Art building on the exposition grounds. (Though, some might argue that Pabst Blue Ribbon beer should be honored with this distinction.)

Jacques Bertillon was Chief of Statistics for the City of Paris. His grandfather, also a noted statistician, had been part of a movement started in 1851 to apply international statistical comparison across a range of subjects, including causes of death. At the 1891 meeting of the movement's main organization, the *International Statistical Institute* (ISI), Bertillon had been tasked with chairing a committee that would compile a list of causes of death, with the expectation that the list would be presented at the 1893 meeting of the ISI in Chicago.

In the report presented in the Palace of Arts, Bertillon included 304 conditions, subdivided into 3 separate lists. Though the original goal had been to list causes of death, the majority of the listed conditions were noted to never or rarely cause death. Most of the conditions were organized into groupings based on the anatomical site of the disease, such as diseases of the circulatory system, diseases of the respiratory system, etc. Some conditions were put into functional or age-related groupings – malformations, diseases of early infancy, diseases of old age, etc.[26] This general categorization system persists to the present day.

Adoption by the ISI of this first systematic and comprehensive compilation of diseases was quickly followed by widespread acceptance. By the time of the ISI's next meeting in 1899, Bertillon's list had been published in English, French, German, and Spanish. The American Public Health Association approved the list in 1897 and recommended adoption of the list as the basis for all vital statistics in North America. By the end of the century, there was growing acceptance of Bertillon's classification across Europe.[27]

---

[25] Ellen Shubart, "World's Columbian Exposition of 1893," Chicago Architecture Center website, accessed June 1, 2025. https://www.architecture.org/online-resources/stories-of-chicago/worlds-columbian-exposition-of-1893

[26] Iwao Moriyama, et al, "History of the Statistical Classification of Diseases and Causes of Death," Centers for Disease Control and Prevention website, accessed May 29, 2025, pp. 9-11 https://www.cdc.gov/nchs/data/misc/classification_diseases2011.pdf

[27] Iwao Moriyama, et al, "History of the Statistical Classification of Diseases and Causes of Death," Centers for Disease Control and Prevention website, accessed May 29, 2025, pp. 12-13 https://www.cdc.gov/nchs/data/misc/classification_diseases2011.pdf

Over the ensuing decades, the list of conditions underwent revisions roughly every decade. Conditions were added, and classifications were adjusted. A numbering system was implemented, making it easier to track the prevalence of conditions and lending itself to a statistical approach to large volumes of records. Through two world wars, a devastating global economic depression, the creation and demise of the League of Nations, and the appearance of the United Nations as a unifying force, the work of the professionals responsible for the list continued almost uninterrupted. It was at the sixth meeting in 1948 that the term *International Classification of Diseases* (ICD) was first used to refer to the document. Other important developments of the 1948 meeting were that 1) the list was first expanded to include causes of morbidity (illness, injury, etc.) in addition to the causes of death that had been its focus since the beginning and 2) the recently established *World Health Organization* (WHO) took charge of the ongoing ICD maintenance responsibility.[28]

The importance of ICD in the world of medical billing cannot be overstated. Before this classification system, the same condition could have different names depending on the practitioner and their location. For example, a physician might write in the medical record "dropsy", while another writes "congestive oedema", while yet another might document "congestive heart failure." Having a standard classification allows the compilation of morbidity and mortality data across a population and, important to billing, an assurance that each of the three doctors mentioned before is treating the same condition.

Insurance Begins to Organize

While the standardization of disease names was being accomplished in the 20th century, there was much work being done to modernize the provision of medical care in the United States. Much of this work had to do with countering the rising cost of healthcare.

During the first three decades of the 1900s, the cost of healthcare rose due to increased consumer demand and higher quality of care from both physicians and hospitals. The American Medical Association had stepped up its credentialing of physicians in the first ten years of the century, and the American College of Surgeons did the same for hospitals beginning in 1913. As demand and quality rose, the charges that could be commanded by physicians and hospitals increased. By 1929, the average

---

[28] Iwao Moriyama, et al, "History of the Statistical Classification of Diseases and Causes of Death," Centers for Disease Control and Prevention website, accessed May 29, 2025, p. 17 https://www.cdc.gov/nchs/data/misc/classification_diseases2011.pdf

American family spent on medical care an annual sum equivalent to almost $2,000 in 21st century terms.[29]

In that same year, a group of teachers employed by the Dallas, Texas school board approached Baylor University Hospital with an intriguing offer. The teachers proposed regular monthly payments of 50 cents each in exchange for up to 21 days of hospital care per person as needed. Baylor agreed, and this type of plan was replicated twenty-five times over the next 8 years. The American Hospital Association gathered these plans into a network to which they affixed the name Blue Cross, a name taken from one of the plans that had formed in Sacramento in 1932. Partly in response to the national emergency that was the Great Depression, when millions of Americans were unable to financially cover medical expenses, the creation of Blue Cross plans was facilitated by state governments who granted them tax-exempt, nonprofit status, thus avoiding burdensome monetary reserve requirements that other insurers bore.[30]

The Great Depression brought to the forefront much of the populist sentiment that had largely gone dormant between the dawn of the new century and the stock market crash of 1929. In response to a suffering public, the U.S. Congress passed the Social Security Act in 1935. There was debate about including healthcare coverage benefits in the Social Security system. However, the bill finally passed with coverage for unemployment compensation and old age assistance but no health coverage.[31] At the same time, the Blue Cross organization recognized that its members needed physician coverage in a prepaid service plan like their hospital service plan.[32]

American physicians as a group saw threats coming from more than one direction – Blue Cross plans might restrict the ability for them to set their own fees, and the federal government might enact a law that called for compulsory national health insurance which would also represent a threat to independent fee setting.

In response to this double threat, a group of physicians started in the late 1930s through the 1940s a network of their own, called Blue Shield, offering physician services that were meant to lie alongside the hospital coverage offered by Blue Cross

---

[29] George Moseley, "The U.S. Health Care Non-System, 1908-2008," *Virtual Mentor* (2008) 10(5): 324-331, https://journalofethics.ama-assn.org/article/us-health-care-non-system-1908-2008/2008-05

[30] Ibid.

[31] History of Blue Cross and Blue Shield, University of North Florida website, accessed June 3, 2025, https://digitalcommons.unf.edu/cgi/viewcontent.cgi?article=3625&context=flablue_text#:~:text=The%20pre%2Dpayment%20movement%20now,eYen%20compete%20with%20each%20other.

[32] George Moseley, "The U.S. Health Care Non-System, 1908-2008," *Virtual Mentor* (2008) 10(5): 324-331, https://journalofethics.ama-assn.org/article/us-health-care-non-system-1908-2008/2008-05

– though it would be 1982 before the two organizations officially came together to form the Blue Cross Blue Shield Association.[33] The emergence of these two entities offered a guiding principle that is foundational for modern medical coding and billing – hospital or facility services are paid separately and distinctly from physician or professional services, often with differing guidelines and philosophies.

It was not only insurance for physician services that arose in the 1940s – other building blocks of modern healthcare financial arrangements were being laid. First was the employer-based model of health insurance. Before the depression, most Americans who had insurance for medical care were insured through a fraternal organization, labor union, or other similar structure.[34] World War II brought government-instituted wage and price controls that meant that employers could not use higher salaries to attract workers. They were, however, allowed to offer non-salary benefits such as health insurance to make sure they had an adequate workforce.[35] In addition to these market forces at work, the Wagner Act of 1935 and the Taft-Hartley Act of 1947 required good faith bargaining around benefits such as health insurance of employers and unions respectively.[36] This further cemented the concept of employer-based health insurance.

Another important development coming out of Congress in the 1940s was the Hill-Burton Act of 1946. The act's formal name was the Hospital Survey and Construction Act, and its provisions began as an initiative of President Truman to improve the nation's health and access to healthcare services, especially for poor and rural areas of the country. By the end of the next thirty years, Hill-Burton had been responsible for the construction of almost one-third of America's hospitals.[37] A

---

[33] History of Blue Cross and Blue Shield, University of North Florida website, accessed June 3, 2025,
https://digitalcommons.unf.edu/cgi/viewcontent.cgi?article=3625&context=flablue_text#:~:text=The%20pre%2Dpayment%20movement%20now,eYen%20compete%20with%20each%20other.

[34] Jennifer Klein *For All These Rights: Business, Labor, and the Shaping of America's Public-Private Welfare State.* Princeton, NJ: Princeton University Press; 2003:204-257.

[35] George Moseley, "The U.S. Health Care Non-System, 1908-2008," *Virtual Mentor* (2008) 10(5): 324-331, https://journalofethics.ama-assn.org/article/us-health-care-non-system-1908-2008/2008-05

[36] 1947 Taft-Hartley Substantive Provisions, National Labor Relations Board website, accessed June 4, 2025, https://www.nlrb.gov/about-nlrb/who-we-are/our-history/1947-taft-hartley-substantive-provisions#:~:text=The%20Taft%2DHartley%20Act%20made,Wagner%20Act%20placed%20on%20employers.

[37] A Bygone Era: When Bipartisanship Led To Health Care Transformation, National Public Radio website, accessed June 5, 2025, https://www.npr.org/sections/health-

number of hospitals in the region where I live, the northeastern portion of Georgia, were "Hill-Burton hospitals".

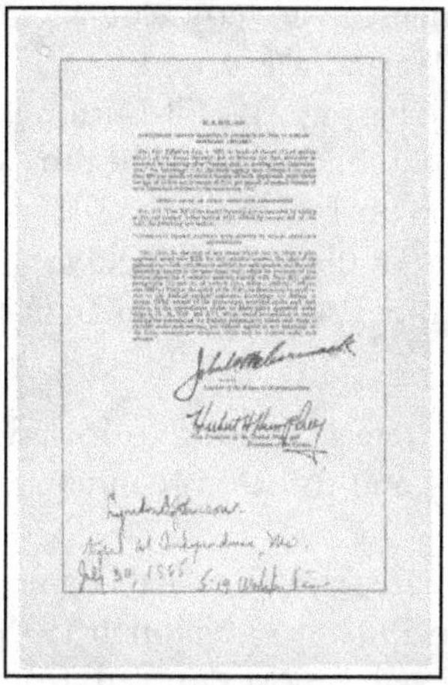

Figure 1: Medicare/Medicaid Act signed by Pres. Johnson, U.S. National Archives and Records Administration.

In addition to building hospitals, the Hill-Burton Act introduced several ideas that remain as guiding principles in healthcare finances even today. One of these is that hospitals who receive federal funds are obligated to care for poor people for free or at low subsidized rates. One of the chief ways that today's non-profit hospitals show evidence of 'community benefit' and thus maintain their tax-exempt status is through the provision of indigent care.[38] At the same time, hospitals struggled with how to meet operating expenses and capital needs while offering this free or discounted treatment – again, a struggle that remains today.

Another important concept embedded in Hill-Burton is that federal funds for healthcare must be matched by state funds. This idea would later become instrumental in the financing of Medicaid.[39]

Medicare, Medicaid, and Rising Costs

The environment created by Blue Cross and Blue Shield, the Hill-Burton Act, and the movement to employer-based health insurance brings us to the cusp of our current modern era. It was into this environment that a monumental law came in the mid 1960s, a law that created the conditions for the evolution of our current medical bills perhaps more than any other. That law was called the Social Security Amendments of 1965, better known as the Medicare and Medicaid Act.

Medicare and Medicaid brought enormous changes to healthcare financial arrangements in the U.S. Before 1965, only about half of the 65 and over American population had health insurance. When Medicare was implemented in 1966, the entire population of Americans aged 65 and up were eligible for Part A hospital services

---

shots/2016/10/02/495775518/a-bygone-era-when-bipartisanship-led-to-health-care-transformation

[38]A Bygone Era: When Bipartisanship Led To Health Care Transformation, National Public Radio website, accessed June 5, 2025, https://www.npr.org/sections/health-shots/2016/10/02/495775518/a-bygone-era-when-bipartisanship-led-to-health-care-transformation

[39] Ibid.

coverage, and almost all signed up for the voluntary Part B physician services coverage.[40]

Financial support of aging Americans had been a goal of many in government since before the passage of the original Social Security Act in 1935 and was on the forefront of President Truman's mind as he pushed for the passage of Hill-Burton in 1946. However, there proved to be insufficient support for publicly funded health insurance for the elderly until President Lyndon B. Johnson pushed through Medicare in the 1960s.[41] Of interest, the ceremonial signing of the law was held in Truman's hometown of Independence, Missouri, with former President Truman in attendance.

Within seven years, recipients of Medicare benefits were expanded to include those who receive disability benefits under Social Security and those with end stage kidney disease, both regardless of age.[42]

Over the first decade of Medicare, the cost of medical care spiraled. Total hospital charges for Medicare beneficiaries rose from $3.4 billion in 1967 to $8 billion in 1973. Over the same timeframe, the average cost for a hospital stay almost doubled, from $657 to $1,228, even as the average length of stay fell. In 1966, a year during which the aging population had Medicare benefits for only half of the year, the per capita spending for hospital care was $445 for each eligible member. In 1975, that number had ballooned to over $1,300.[43]

Before the twentieth anniversary of Medicare, American health spending had risen from a 1965 value of 6% of *gross national product* (GDP) to a 1984 value of 10.6% of GDP. Among the reasons for this healthcare inflation were 1) payment methodologies that incentivized healthcare providers to increase charges, and 2) expectations among the American public that they have ready access to quality medical care.[44]

Hospitalization rates continued to climb, as both physicians and patients took advantage of their financing options to push the limits of quality and amount of care

---

[40] Marian Gornick, et. al. "Thirty Years of Medicare: Impact on the Covered Population," *Health Care Financing Review* (1996) Winter;18(2):179–237. https://pmc.ncbi.nlm.nih.gov/articles/PMC4193632/

[41] CMS' program history, Centers for Medicare and Medicaid Services website, accessed June 5, 2025, https://www.cms.gov/about-cms/who-we-are/history

[42] CMS' program history, Centers for Medicare and Medicaid Services website, accessed June 5, 2025, https://www.cms.gov/about-cms/who-we-are/history

[43] Marian Gornick, "Ten Years of Medicare: Impact on the Covered Population," *Social Security Bulletin* (1976) 39(7):3–21.

[44] Marian Gornick, et. al. "Thirty Years of Medicare: Impact on the Covered Population," *Health Care Financing Review* (1996) Winter;18(2):179–237. https://pmc.ncbi.nlm.nih.gov/articles/PMC4193632/

higher. Medicare payment methods were certainly favorable to healthcare providers. At the outset in 1966, hospitals were paid whatever costs they listed on the claim form plus 2% for non-profits and 1.5% for for-profits. The percentages paid above listed costs were termed "*return on capital*" (ROC) payments and were intended to help fund hospital expansion. Though ROC payments were eliminated in 1969, a replacement payment called a "nursing differential" added 8.5% of routine inpatient nursing salary costs.[45]

As the 1980s began, inpatient hospitalizations continued to increase annually, stretching an already tight budget. During Medicare's first two decades, the rate of growth of Part A – and Part B – payments greatly exceeded the rate of general inflation.[46] It became clear that guardrails needed to be put into place.

The early 1980s were tumultuous. The Iran hostage crisis was unfolding, only resolving just as Ronald Reagan took office in January of 1981. Reagan rode to office, not on a horse like one of his movie characters, but on a wave of religious fervor among conservative evangelical voters. Some of them referred to Reagan's surviving an assassination attempt in March 1981 as an "act of God". However, in 1983, it was not an act of God that finally seemed to stem the tide of spending on inpatient stays by changing the way hospital claims are submitted.

It was an act of Congress.

---

[45] Stephen Weiner, "'Reasonable Cost' Reimbursement for Inpatient Hospital Services Under Medicare and Medicaid: The Emergence of Public Control," *American Journal of Law & Medicine* (1977) 3(1):1-47. https://www.cambridge.org/core/journals/american-journal-of-law-and-medicine/article/abs/reasonable-cost-reimbursement-for-inpatient-hospital-services-under-medicare-and-medicaid-the-emergence-of-public-control/72F2BA5DA901597E6BD3FEF8FF19C339

[46] Marian Gornick, et. al. "Thirty Years of Medicare: Impact on the Covered Population," *Health Care Financing Review* (1996) Winter;18(2):179–237. https://pmc.ncbi.nlm.nih.gov/articles/PMC4193632/

Chapter 2: Breadcrumbs for the Labyrinth

- The close of the 1800s brought a scientific approach to the naming and categorization of disease states, making the statistical analysis of population health possible.
- The approach to nomenclature and classification was improved throughout the 20th century – eventually becoming the International Classification of Diseases or ICD – and enhancements continue today.
- Health insurance coverage for Americans dramatically changed with the rise of Blue Cross and Blue Shield plans in the 1930s and 1940s.
- In the last half of the 20th century, employer-based health insurance became the predominant way that Americans paid for medical care.
- The Hill-Burton Act of 1946 considerably increased the number of hospitals in the U.S.
- Hill-Burton also placed a requirement on hospitals to offer indigent care. Hospitals were forced to look elsewhere for revenue to offset this expense.

CHAPTER 3

THE FUTURE BECOMES THE PRESENT

Harold's belly is hurting.

He woke up this Thursday morning, September 22, 1983, with some nausea and within an hour or so developed pain low on his right side. As the pain worsens, he decides to go see his doctor who promptly diagnoses appendicitis.

His doctor consults a surgeon, and Harold has his appendix removed that very day. He is told to expect to remain in the hospital for several days and is instructed to stay in bed at all times and to call for a nurse if he needs assistance. Over the next week, he is given pain medication, intravenous antibiotics and fluids, and nursing care such as changing the dressing on his surgical incision. The next Monday, Harold's twin brother Lawrence – yes, their parents called them Harry and Larry - visits him in the hospital because that day, September 26, is their 66th birthday.

Harold remains in the hospital until Friday, September 30. At discharge, a hospital claim is prepared which itemizes multiple charges:

- Room and board (an entry for each day),
- Laboratory tests,
- Pharmacy charges,
- Radiology charges,
- Operating room charges, and
- Other professional services.

The total billed charges add up to $3,390.

By coincidence, Lawrence starts to have the same kind of pain as Harold and goes to the same doctor on Monday, October 3, 1983. Lawrence is, like Harold, diagnosed with appendicitis, is admitted to the same hospital, and undergoes an appendectomy later on Monday performed by the same surgeon as Harold's.

The hospital has a new clinical protocol, just rolled out over the weekend, that calls for walking in the hallway the evening after surgery. On the day after surgery, Lawrence is taught how to change the dressing on his incision and is given liquids to drink in the morning and soft food in the evening.

On the next day, Wednesday, October 5, Lawrence is discharged. His claim is prepared, and it lists three items:

- a diagnosis code (540.0, acute appendicitis),
- a procedure code (47.0, appendectomy), and
- a DRG designation (167, appendectomy without complications).

The total billed charge - $2,451 based on the relative weight of DRG 167.[47]

Prospective Payment Arrives

On April 20, 1983, President Ronald Reagan signed into law an amendment to the Social Security Act that made significant changes to Social Security. However, one of its most enduring legacies is the creation of the Medicare *prospective payment system* (PPS). The PPS went into effect on October 1, 1983, and thus hospitals were required to begin submitting a different kind of claim form beginning on that date.

The PPS was instituted in response to the ongoing rise in healthcare spending. In the ten-year period ending in 1982, American national expenditures for healthcare had risen about 13% per year. Though the 1982-1990 rate of growth was projected to be slightly lower, national expenditure annual growth was still projected to reach almost 10%, with the federal government responsible for around 30% of all healthcare spending. With the American population 75 years of age or over projected to increase four times as fast as the average annual rate for persons under 65 years of age, federal leaders felt that something had to be done to control healthcare outlays.[48]

The PPS (eventually termed the IPPS, or *inpatient prospective payment system*, to distinguish it from the later outpatient system) made use of an innovation first developed at Yale University – the *diagnostic related group* (DRG) system.

DRGs were initially intended to be a way to monitor the quality of care and to help determine the quantity and level of services being utilized in the hospital setting. The DRG system was first used for reimbursement purposes by the New Jersey Department of Health who paid hospitals a fixed amount, tied to the DRG, for each patient that was treated. The mostly successful roll out of a PPS using DRGs in New Jersey led to the national PPS, for all Medicare patients, in 1983.[49]

---

[47] Harry and Larry are fictitious, and their hospital bills are estimates based on:
Mary Moien, "Patient charges in short-stay hospitals United States-1968-1970," *Vital Health Stat* (1974) 15:1-47. https://www.cdc.gov/nchs/data/series/sr_13/sr13_015acc.pdf
and
Mark Freeland, "Health spending in the 1980's: integration of clinical practice patterns with management," *Health Care Financing Review* (1984) 5(3):1-68.
It is highly unlikely that a hospital changed their protocols so drastically within a few days after PPS was instituted, but this scenario helps to make the point about the monumental change in processes to come.

[48] Mark Freeland, "Health spending in the 1980's: integration of clinical practice patterns with management," *Health Care Financing Review* (1984) 5(3):1-68.

[49] Design and development of the Diagnosis Related Group, Centers for Medicare and Medicaid Services website, accessed June 7, 2025,

We finally come to an example of the distinction between the philosophies held in previous eras (discussed in Chapters 1 and 2) and the modern era in regard to access to and payment for healthcare. Remember from Chapter 2 that the Blue Cross Blue Shield experience helped to establish separate payment methods and philosophies for hospital (referred to as facility) charges and physician (referred to as professional) charges. As we continue our discussion of the IPPS and other payment methods for inpatient stays, keep in mind that we are considering only hospital or facility charges. Physician charges will be explored in Chapter 5, as will outpatient claims.

American government leaders in the 1970s were faced with determining how to pay hospitals as the cost of their services had been rising for a decade and saw no signs of slowing their growth. If the philosophies prevalent in the Middle Ages through the 1800s were followed, hospitals who served richer patients would be paid more while those who served poorer populations would be paid less. However, now that Medicare was the healthcare payer for all older Americans regardless of their wealth, this model does not hold up. Of course, it is also inconsistent with the American principles of equality – not that we as a nation always uphold those.

As early as 1977, leaders at the newly formed *Health Care Financing Administration* (HCFA) along with President Carter's *Health, Education, and Welfare* (HEW) Secretary Joseph Califano recognized the spiraling healthcare costs we have already discussed and concluded that physicians and hospitals were being improperly paid.[50] The existing fee-for-service system allowed healthcare providers to bill whatever they wanted. There was no incentive to try to contain costs – in other words, the providers had no skin in the game.

Based on groundwork laid by Yale professors John Thompson and Robert Fetter in the 1960s and 1970s, the PPS initiated in 1983 shifted the responsibility for efficiency to hospitals.[51] Providers certainly now had significant skin in the game.

How DRGs Measure a Hospital Stay

There are many factors in the PPS that determine how much a hospital is paid to treat a patient's condition. As we explore each of these factors and discover their interplay, remember that DRGs are a part of the *inpatient* PPS – they are not used to

---

https://www.cms.gov/icd10m/version37-fullcode-cms/fullcode_cms/Design_and_development_of_the_Diagnosis_Related_Group_(DRGs).pdf#

[50] Robert Derzon, "The Genesis of HCFA," *Health Affairs* (2005) 24:Suppl1.

[51] Jon Chilingerian, "Origins of DRGs in the United States: A technical, political and cultural story," *Globalization of Managerial Innovation in Health Care* (2008) 4-33. https://www.researchgate.net/publication/286656118_Origins_of_DRGs_in_the_United_States_A_technical_political_and_cultural_story

calculate payments for outpatient services. (We will discuss the outpatient PPS in Chapter 4.) Also, realize that the PPS rolled out in 1983 was aimed at *Medicare* claims. The initially published DRGs were meant for an elderly population. Even now, it should not be assumed that all independently available commercial health insurance plans and employer-based plans are covered by a PPS, though some are. For example, most if not all commercially available Medicare Advantage plans in present day utilize DRGs for inpatient claims.

In developing and utilizing DRGs, the Yale professors and the bureaucrats coming after them recognized that the existing ways to explain cost differences between hospitals were insufficient. Up until then, such factors as the number of beds in the hospital or the hospital's status as a teaching hospital were used in an attempt to funnel additional money to the facilities where it was most needed. However, factors such as these did not adequately identify need. For example, a tiny hospital – which was assumed to have more need for financial support than a very large hospital – might be in a very affluent area and may treat patients who have generally mild or moderate medical conditions, while the large hospital might serve a sizeable indigent community with very severe medical conditions.

Patient factors that affect the cost of medical care are collectively called the "case mix." In distinction to previous patient classification systems, DRGs offered the first widely implemented way to define and measure case mix.[52]

In its original iteration, the DRG system segmented 10,000 ICD-9 principal diagnosis codes into *Major Diagnostic Categories* (MDCs) and then used three variables to determine different levels of resource consumption: 1) the presence or absence of surgical procedures during the hospitalization, 2) the presence of complications or co-morbidities (coexisting conditions that may or may not affect the care of the patient), and 3) the patient's age.[53]

Even when only considering the principal diagnosis and these three factors, a dizzying array of possibilities resulted. For example, one MDC – diseases and disorders of the kidney and urinary tract – had at least 14 different DRGs just for the subsegment dealing with those hospitalizations with a surgical procedure.

In the years after the initial introduction of basic DRGs, it became clear that the DRG system as it existed provided at best a crude approximation of resource utilization. Other factors were thus added to the calculation. In 2007, the *Medical (or Medicare) Severity DRG* (MS-DRG) system was rolled out by CMS (Centers for

---

[52] Jon Chilingerian, "Origins of DRGs in the United States: A technical, political and cultural story," *Globalization of Managerial Innovation in Health Care* (2008) 4-33. https://www.researchgate.net/publication/286656118_Origins_of_DRGs_in_the_United_States_A_technical_political_and_cultural_story

[53] Ibid

Medicare and Medicaid Services).[54] Under this new system and its revisions over a several year period, the three categories were expanded, and new details were added:

1) Surgical procedures still held an important role in determining the DRG.
2) The patient's age still mattered.
3) Some co-morbidities were designated as *complicating conditions* (CCs) or *major complicating conditions* (MCCs). If a co-morbidity did not typically affect a patient's care, it was not designated as a CC or MCC.
4) A "*present on admission*" (POA) indicator was added for each diagnosis. If a coded condition was acquired while the patient was already in the hospital, the POA indicator was entered as "N", and that condition might not be included in the calculation of the DRG, depending on the specific algorithm.
5) The disposition code on the claim (for example, discharged to home, transferred to another facility, etc.) also affected the payment, though it did not typically directly affect the choice of DRG.

With these additional considerations, the number of DRGs rose from the initial number of 467 in 1983 to over 750 in 2007.[55]

Before looking at how DRG systems continued to evolve after the basic DRG was implemented in 1983, let's consider an example that illustrates how the MS-DRG system – the system that was the direct offshoot of the initial basic DRG system – intends to estimate the cost of caring for a patient.

Imagine a 68-year-old woman named Alice who is admitted in current times to the hospital with shortness of breath. She has no significant medical history other than high blood pressure controlled with medications and a blood sugar that has been mildly elevated on her annual physical for the past few years.

The X-ray of her chest showed what the radiologist terms as "mild vascular congestion". Alice's doctor orders an intravenous diuretic medication and some laboratory tests. By the next day, she is feeling better and is discharged home.

The doctor documents a diagnosis of acute congestive heart failure in the medical record. The hospital's medical coder reviews the record and enters ICD-10 code I11.0 (hypertension with heart failure) as the principal diagnosis on the claim. Other secondary diagnosis codes are also entered – I50.21 (acute congestive heart failure)

---

[54] Nancy Reading, "CDIP, MCC, CC, HCC: The Road to Better Revenue," American Academy of Professional Coders website, January 1, 2010, accessed June 9, 2025, https://www.aapc.com/blog/25741-cdip-mcc-cc-hcc-the-road-to-better-revenue/

[55] Jon Chilingerian, "Origins of DRGs in the United States: A technical, political and cultural story," *Globalization of Managerial Innovation in Health Care* (2008) 4-33. https://www.researchgate.net/publication/286656118_Origins_of_DRGs_in_the_United_States_A_technical_political_and_cultural_story

and R73.9 (high blood sugar, unspecified).[56] The coder enters POA indicator "Y" for all diagnosis codes since Alice had congestive heart failure at the time of her admission and has had high blood sugars for months. The disposition code is 01, meaning that Alice was discharged to home.

Modern medical coding makes use of computer programs and platforms called encoders that automatically apply all of the various rules and guidelines to arrive at the correct DRG. The coder enters all of the pertinent elements (diagnosis and procedure codes, disposition code, etc. and the encoder enters the code for the DRG.

Based on Alice's information, the DRG is calculated to be MS-DRG 293 (heart failure and shock without CC/MCC). The relative weight for this admission is 0.5615, corresponding to a payment of around $3,500. If there had been a CC on the claim – like J44.1 (chronic obstructive pulmonary disease with acute exacerbation) – the paid amount would have been almost $5,800. By comparison, the MS-DRG for minor small and large bowel procedures without CC/MCC carries a relative weight more than twice as large (1.2878) with a payment of over $8,000 – thus demonstrating the skewing of payment amounts by the presence of a surgical procedure.[57]

In Chapter 5, we will explore the risk for misuse and abuse of these codes. For now, notice that simply adding one diagnosis code to the claim results in a 65% increase in the paid amount.

Severity, Risk, and New DRG Systems

As complicated as the MS-DRG system is, with over 700 possible DRGs and sometimes several claim elements determining the proper DRG and thus the paid amount, DRG systems that emerged in the decade after the initial 1983 release of basic DRGs are much more complex.

As was mentioned before, the basic DRGs released in 1983 were clearly skewed toward older patients. Even with annual revisions in the PPS, there were few if any changes in a given year geared toward pediatric or obstetrical diagnoses. At the same time, more and more entities were making use of the PPS for various purposes: hospitals for internal management systems, state Medicaid departments and Blue Cross organizations for payments, state data commissions for comparative reporting systems, etc.[58] It was becoming clear that either significant revisions to the existing DRG system were needed or a whole new system was required.

---

[56] ICD-10-CM Expert (2025) American Academy of Professional Coders, Alphabetical and Tabular Indices.

[57] DRG Expert – Volume 1 (2025) Optum 360, p. xxiii.

[58] All Patient Refined Diagnosis Related Groups (APR-DRGs), Agency for Healthcare Research and Quality website (2003) Accessed June 9, 2025, https://hcup-us.ahrq.gov/db/nation/nis/APR-DRGsV20MethodologyOverviewandBibliography.pdf

The state of New York passed legislation in 1987 that called for the DRG system to take into account newborns and people with HIV infections. In response, the New York State Department of Health contracted with the 3M corporation to make the necessary changes in DRG definitions and software. The result was the *All Patient DRG system* or AP-DRG.

AP-DRGs introduced new variables into the DRG calculation, including birth weight for newborns and the duration of mechanical ventilation. AP-DRGs, like basic DRGs before them, had relative weights based solely on estimated average resource intensity for each group of diagnoses. Neither system attempted to offer more detail about medical conditions.[59]

During the 1980s, there was increasing demand for a classification system that would allow comparison of hospitals' differing resource and outcome measures and that would facilitate management of increasingly common capitated payment arrangements. A new DRG system, called *All Patient Refined DRGs* or APR-DRG, introduced in 1990 fulfilled these needs. In addition to resource intensity, APR-DRGs added two factors:

1) *Severity of illness* (SOI) – an approximation of the patient's loss of bodily or organ function, and
2) Risk of mortality – the likelihood of the patient's dying.[60]

Because of APR-DRG's applicability to pediatric and obstetrical populations and with its more detailed tiering of diagnostic groups, APR-DRGs became the most widely used system for state Medicaid agencies. Currently, there are 330 base DRGs in APR-DRG, with each DRG (and each ICD code) also having an SOI indicator of 1-4. Thus, there are 1,320 total APR-DRGs.

The SOI indicator for each ICD code and the overall SOI for each DRG are important determinants of the relative weight and the paid amount of each claim. Unlike in MS-DRG where the relative weight is mostly affected only by one or two diagnoses on the claim – the principal diagnosis and the presence of either a CC or an MCC – APR-DRG gives weight to almost all of the diagnoses on the claim. The principal diagnosis, along with the principal procedure if applicable, determines the base APR-DRG, while the secondary diagnoses and procedures affect the overall DRG SOI.

---

[59] All Patient Refined Diagnosis Related Groups (APR-DRGs), Agency for Healthcare Research and Quality website (2003) Accessed June 9, 2025, https://hcup-us.ahrq.gov/db/nation/nis/APR-DRGsV20MethodologyOverviewandBibliography.pdf

[60] Ibid.

Let's look at an example from earlier days in APR-DRG to see this interplay of factors. Imagine two different patients, both admitted to the hospital for treatment of congestive heart failure. (See the following chart.)

Principal Diagnosis – Congestive Heart Failure		
	Patient 1	Patient 2
Secondary Diagnoses	• Chronic Obstructive Pulmonary Disease • Atrial Fibrillation	• Chronic Obstructive Pulmonary Disease • Atrial Fibrillation • Acute Respiratory Failure • Acidosis • Decubitus Ulcer • Malnutrition • Cardiogenic Shock
APR-DRG	194 (Heart Failure)	194 (Heart Failure)
APR-DRG SOI	2 - Moderate	4 – Extreme
Average Cost in NY in 2007	$7,087	$24,616

Adapted from Blue Cross Blue Shield Tennessee website, https://www.bcbst.com/providers/webinar/APRDRG.pdf

Both patients have the same principal diagnosis and two of the same secondary diagnoses. Given just that information, the SOI is calculated to be 2, thus being of moderate severity.

However, Patient 2 has a number of additional diagnoses, many of them indicating relatively severe disease (acute respiratory failure, acidosis, cardiogenic shock, etc.) and thus each of those secondary diagnoses adding to the SOI. The SOI of the second claim is 4, the extreme level of severity, and thus the payment is more than triple the amount of the first claim.

The costs or paid amounts, like the ones in the chart, are calculated by multiplying the relative weight of the DRG by the hospital's base rate. CMS assigns the base rate for each hospital that treats Medicare patients, and the rate is based on such elements as the average wages paid in the hospital's region, the facility's percentage of low-income patients, and whether or not the hospital is a teaching hospital.[61]

In Chapter 5, we will explore the details of how CCs and MCCs in the MS-DRG system and SOIs in the APR-DRG system have created something of a battlefield on which providers and payers slug it out.

For now, let me close out talking about inpatient claims by pointing out that some payers do not use any type of PPS in paying claims. There are other payment methodologies in use that differ greatly from PPS.

Other Ways to Pay

In the percent-of-charges method, the total charges on the claim are multiplied by a contracted percentage agreed upon by the provider and the payer. Though less

---

[61] Acute Inpatient PPS, Centers for Medicare and Medicaid Services website, accessed June 14, 2025, https://www.cms.gov/medicare/payment/prospective-payment-systems/acute-inpatient-pps

common now than in the past, this method is still in use by some non-governmental payers.[62]

Cost-plus pricing was first made popular by Blue Cross plans and is still in use today by some self-funded and consumer-directed health plans. Typically, the health plan using this method bases its fee schedule for providers on Medicare, to set the cost basis, and then adds a pre-determined margin in the range of 15% to 20% over the Medicare amount.[63]

The evolution of inpatient billing and coding structures that we have seen in this chapter explains some of the complexity that we see when trying to understand our own healthcare claims. The truth is that the system is complicated for everyone, not just patients. Imagine the hospital administrator dealing with multiple payment methodologies – APR-DRG for Medicaid patients, MS-DRG for Medicare patients, perhaps percent-of-charges or cost-plus pricing for yet another group of patients – and you can begin to see that this complexity can become overwhelming. Even the claims processing staff in payer organizations find the blizzard of diagnosis and procedure codes and related coding rules and guidelines bewildering.

The early 90s found the federal government looking back with some satisfaction on the changes made to the Medicare inpatient claims process. Since the introduction of DRGs in 1983, there had been decreases in average length of stay, total number of hospitalizations, and costs per admission.[64] Several states and non-governmental payers had adopted DRGs as a payment methodology for inpatient stays.

Feeling confident, the U.S. government shifted its gaze. Now, in its crosshairs would be outpatient claims and that most politically dangerous target of all – physician services.

---

[62] Percent of charges and per diem rates, Revenue Cycle Advisor website, accessed June 10, 2025, https://revenuecycleadvisor.com/news-analysis/qa-percent-charges-and-diem-rates

[63] Reference Based Pricing, Diversified Group website, accessed June 10, 2025, https://www.dgb-online.com/cost-plus/

[64] Jon Chilingerian, "Origins of DRGs in the United States: A technical, political and cultural story," *Globalization of Managerial Innovation in Health Care* (2008) p. 18. https://www.researchgate.net/publication/286656118_Origins_of_DRGs_in_the_United_States_A_technical_political_and_cultural_story

Chapter 3: Breadcrumbs for the Labyrinth

- The Medicare prospective payment system, introduced in 1983, changed inpatient hospital payment from retrospective cost-based reimbursement to a predetermined payment tied to the patient's clinical category.
- Diagnosis Related Groups, or DRGs, use documented diagnoses, procedures, and patient factors to approximate the resources required for an inpatient stay.
- The DRG system shifted financial risk toward hospitals and created strong incentives to manage length of stay, resource use, and documentation accuracy.
- MS-DRGs added greater emphasis on complications and comorbidities, especially CCs and MCCs, making one supported or unsupported secondary diagnosis capable of substantially changing payment.
- Present-on-admission indicators, discharge disposition, hospital base rates, wage adjustments, teaching status, and low-income patient factors can all affect final payment.
- APR-DRGs expanded the grouping concept beyond the elderly Medicare population and added severity of illness and risk of mortality, making the system especially useful for Medicaid and all-patient populations.
- Prospective payment improved cost control but also made the coded claim a financial battlefield where documentation and coding precision matter enormously.

CHAPTER 4
THE ARITHMETIC OF HEALING

Peggy really likes her job, and she's good at it – even with all the change that is happening. She has worked as a claims processor for the past ten years at the Columbus Plan, in Columbus, Georgia. Her organization offers Blue Cross Blue Shield health insurance plans to people in the southern part of her state. A few months ago, in early 1966, the Columbus Plan merged with the Savannah Plan,[65] and now Peggy hears that a new system to report claims is on its way. So much change!

Peggy's coworkers can hardly believe how quickly she can decipher the written and typed claims that flow into the office each day. Peggy glances over the descriptions of procedures on the claim forms and almost immediately knows which procedure is being described, even though the explanations vary greatly between claims. This form may say "cholecystectomy" while another may document "gallbladder removal" while a third might say "extraction of cholecyst". Peggy knows that each term describes the same operation.

The new claim reporting system is coming from the *American Medical Association* (AMA), and Peggy understands that each surgical procedure will have its own code. No more squinting and trying to decide what is written on the claim form.

Peggy smiles and thinks, They thought I was fast before! Just wait until those CPTs come out!

Physician Fees and Professional Autonomy

The way that physicians are paid for their work in the United States has been a sticky subject for a long time. Harkening back to the customs in medieval Europe that were explored in Chapter 1, American physicians through the 19th century and well into the 20th century held to the practice of setting their fees as they saw fit while attempting to always balance the "making health" side of their profession with the "making

[65] Georgia Historical Society Names Anthem Blue Cross and Blue Shield of Georgia Newest Honoree in Georgia Business History Initiative, Georgia Historical Society website, accessed June 10, 2025, https://www.georgiahistory.com/georgia-historical-society-names-anthem-blue-cross-and-blue-shield-of-georgia-newest-honoree-in-georgia-business-history-initiative/#

money" side.[66] As was common among English physicians before them, American doctors freely used sliding scales and thus charged patients what the patient was felt to be able to afford. One example from 1931 shows that a physician's charge for managing diabetes ranged from $232 to over $1,000, depending on the patient's socioeconomic status. It was common practice for a surgeon to charge one month of the patient's salary for a major operation, a convenient way to utilize a sliding scale.[67]

Physicians' freedom to set their own charges was tied up in their view of their profession as a whole. Doctors, they felt, are expected to govern themselves and as such deserve the respect given to the profession. All of this was linked to the view, from ancient times, that physicians have a duty to serve humankind. As summed up in the AMA 1923 Code of Ethics, "A profession has for its prime object the service it can render to humanity; reward or financial gain should be a subordinate consideration."[68]

The American physician's duty and right to self-govern in the financial realm were not only customs of the profession – they were also upheld by the courts. Specifically in regard to sliding scale fees, a 1931 California court ruling said that "there is evidence of a recognized usage, which has grown into a custom, to graduate professional charges with reference to the financial condition of the patient...."[69] Through this ruling and others, the courts determined that the patient's legal obligation to pay was implicit, and the standard for setting fees was that charges are "usual, customary, and reasonable"[70] – a standard that remained in effect for decades and still guides some fee-setting today.

This ancient tradition of professional autonomy began to be challenged in the early 1900s. In 1906, the American Association of Labor Legislation (AALL) initiated a campaign to push for a national health insurance program that would benefit the working class and those earning less than $1,200 per year, including their dependents. Initially, the AMA joined the AALL in supporting this program.

However, as details of the proposed legislation filtered down to state medical societies, opposition to the program grew. It was not clear at all as to how physicians would be paid in a national health insurance plan, and there was growing concern

---

[66] Mark Hall, et al, Learning from the Legal History of Billing for Medical Fees, *Journal of General Internal Medicine* (2008) 23(8):1257–60

[67] Mark Hall, et al, Learning from the Legal History of Billing for Medical Fees, *Journal of General Internal Medicine* (2008) 23(8):1257–60

[68] Principles of Medical Ethics of the American Medical Association. This language remained in the "Principles" until the 1957 revision.

[69] Mark Hall, et al, Learning from the Legal History of Billing for Medical Fees, *Journal of General Internal Medicine* (2008) 23(8):1257–60

[70] Ibid.

about an erosion in autonomy for doctors. Eventually, the AMA flipped its position of support, later denying that it had ever supported the legislation in the first place.[71]

At the same time, disapproval of a national health plan was expressed by, understandably, the private insurance industry and by the American Federation of Labor, who saw a national health plan as an example of unwelcome government supervision of workers' lives. Opposition was amplified, with America's entry into World War I, by anti-socialist sentiment that swept across the nation.[72]

The momentum toward national health insurance that swelled in the years around 1910 faded, only to surge again in the 1930s and 1940s. However, again due partly to opposition from the AMA, the Social Security Act of 1935, the Wagner National Health Act of 1939, and the Hill-Burton Act of 1946 – all meant to bring some type of national health coverage – had any provision for national health insurance scrubbed from their pages before passage.[73]

Over the first half of the 20th century, the AMA became a formidable political force, one that wielded great influence among policymakers. It is estimated that, by the early 1950s, around 75% of American physicians were AMA members.[74] In 1948, the AMA raised its dues to contract with the nation's first professional lobbyist firm to successfully counter President Truman's push for national health insurance.[75] One can only assume that many politicians felt the physician lobby was too strong to safely oppose.

However, by the mid-1960s, things were rapidly changing. Largely pushed forward by a grass-roots movement, a national health insurance plan was finally implemented in 1965 – albeit on a relatively narrow scale – with the passage of the Medicare and Medicaid Act. With the government now paying the bills for an important subset of American patients, it became clear that a standard means of reporting the work of physicians must be devised, and it only made sense that the nation's physicians – under the aegis of the AMA – be the ones to devise it.

---

[71] Karen Palmer, A Brief History: Universal Health Care Efforts in the U.S., Physicians for a National Health Program website (1999) Accessed June 11, 2025, https://pnhp.org/a-brief-history-universal-health-care-efforts-in-the-us/

[72] Karen Palmer, A Brief History: Universal Health Care Efforts in the U.S., Physicians for a National Health Program website (1999) Accessed June 11, 2025, https://pnhp.org/a-brief-history-universal-health-care-efforts-in-the-us/

[73] Ibid.

[74] American Medical Association, Influence Watch website, accessed June 11, 2025, https://www.influencewatch.org/non-profit/american-medical-association/#

[75] Jonathan Michels, "The Spin Doctors," Jacobin website, accessed June 11, 2025, https://jacobin.com/2020/01/american-medical-association-medicare-for-all

CPT Creates a Common Language

Like the ICD before it, AMA's *Current Procedural Terminology* (CPT) system was intended to standardize the names of procedures and other healthcare services. One AMA physician wrote in 1964 that medical terminology of that era was "colored with hearsay and superstition, tangled and distorted in whimsical narrative." He went on to say that medical terms must be standardized to prevent medical practice from becoming "stagnant and detached."[76]

The Medicare and Medicaid Act of 1965 included provisions for Part A, to cover hospital costs, and Part B, to cover physician and outpatient services. As we discuss CPT codes, keep in mind that we will address CPT codes used for outpatient claims. The current inpatient PPS uses a different coding system for inpatient claims – the ICD-10 procedure coding system or ICD-10-PCS.

For the first 25 years of Medicare, the Part B paid amount for each CPT code was based on the concept of "customary, prevailing, and reasonable" (CPR) charges. CPR was defined by the Medicare program as: 1) *customary* – the median of an individual physician's charges for a particular service for a defined period of time, 2) *prevailing* - at the 90th percentile of the usual charges of all same-specialty physicians in a defined Medicare payment area, and 3) *reasonable* – the lowest of the physician's actual payment for the service, that physician's usual charge, or the most common charge in the area.[77]

There were several problems with the CPR method of calculating prices. First, the system allowed for vast differences in payments for the same service, as a careful perusal of the above CPR definitions will reveal. Another problem was that the insurance companies that processed Part B claims had their own internal policies that further affected the amount paid for services. Because of these and other factors, wide variations in Medicare payment levels between different regions and physician specialties developed.[78]

Dissatisfaction with this variation in payments, on the part of both physicians and the government, resulted in several initiatives in the 1970s and 1980s, but the problem persisted. The introduction of the inpatient PPS in 1983, with a seeming resolution of

---

[76] Confusing names for Disease 'Hinder' Progress, Journal of the American Medical Association (1964) 190 (7): 39, https://jamanetwork.com/journals/jama/article-abstract/1165418

[77] Development of the Resource-Based Relative Value Scale, American Medical Association website, accessed June 11, 2025, https://www.ama-assn.org/system/files/development-of-the-resource-based-relative-value-scale.pdf

[78] Development of the Resource-Based Relative Value Scale, American Medical Association website, accessed June 11, 2025, https://www.ama-assn.org/system/files/development-of-the-resource-based-relative-value-scale.pdf

the overpayment issue for hospitalizations, turned a great deal of attention on physician services payments. In the late 1980s, Harvard University led a research study into a *resource-based relative value scale* (RBRVS) payment schedule. With the support of the AMA, the federal government implemented RBRVS as the basis for setting fees for CPTs in 1992.

Relative Value and the Price of Work

Under RBRVS, each CPT is evaluated in part by the *Relative value scale Update Committee (*RUC). The RUC is composed of physician representatives from 22 major national medical specialty societies and other personnel.[79] For each CPT code, the RUC decides on the relative value, upon which the Medicare payment amount is based. Three components go into the calculation: amount of physician work required by the procedure or service, the expenses borne by the practice, and the malpractice insurance expense.[80] The RUC makes its recommendations to CMS, but the final decision is made by the government.

The initial 1966 edition was focused on surgery and included 3,500 4-digit codes.[81] Over time, the CPT manual expanded to cover radiology, anesthesia, pathology, and general medical procedures and services. Today, the number of codes has increased to over 11,000.

In addition to the complexity brought by 11,000 codes, a confusing collection of rules and guidelines have arisen over the past decades. One example is the large number of rules around bundling.

Bundling, Modifiers, and HCPCS

Bundling of services on a medical claim means that two or more services are all included in the charge for the main service instead of each being paid separately – though there could be other services that are not included, and thus it would be acceptable to include those on the claim.

Let's take a non-medical example. Say you go to your favorite fancy restaurant and order a nice steak dinner. You expect to be charged for the steak itself, any extra sides, and the wine that you ordered. However, you do not expect to have a line on your dinner check for the chair in which you sit, the table that holds your food, the

---

[79] Composition of the RVS Update Committee (RUC), American Medical Association website, accessed June 11, 2025, https://www.ama-assn.org/about/rvs-update-committee-ruc/composition-rvs-update-committee-ruc

[80] Work RVU Calculator (Relative Value Units), American Academy of Professional Coders website, accessed June 11, 2025, https://www.aapc.com/tools/rvu-calculator.aspx

[81] The Basics of CPT, Applied Policy website, accessed June 11, 2025, https://www.appliedpolicy.com/the-basics-of-cpt/

host who shows you to the table, the bus staff who cleans your table, or the air you breathe.

Now, let's look at a simple medical example. CPT code 36400[82] is used to report the insertion of an intravenous catheter into a vein to inject something. Sometimes, that it is a separately reportable procedure – in other words, sometimes that is paid a certain fee (established by the RUC process described before) even when other procedures are done. However, when CPT code 79101 is used to report the injection of a radioactive drug used to treat cancer (a radiopharmaceutical), coding rules state that CPT 36400 is not to be entered on the claim. This is because the insertion of the intravenous catheter is already included in the price of the radiopharmaceutical injection. If the patient was also given an intravenous injection of steroids during the same treatment session, it is acceptable to enter CPT 96374 (intravenous injection of a therapeutic substance) on the claim since the steroid injection is not bundled with the radiopharmaceutical injection.

You might wonder how a medical coder keeps up with all these rules. In the days before the computerized coding systems, it was indeed difficult and required coders to keep the CPT manual close at hand to look up possible conflicts on the claim. Now, coders can enter the procedure description and have the code entered – or even better, have the code itself auto-populate directly from the electronic medical record (EMR). The coding software then automatically takes into account coding rules and alerts the coder to questionable codes on the claim.

However, even though computerized coding systems alert coders to conflicts in the codes, it is easy to ignore the alerts because coding rules frequently change, and they are not uniformly enforced. Another variable comes with the use of modifiers.

Modifiers are used to indicate exceptions to existing coding rules. For example, CPT coding guidelines say that most outpatient procedure codes have bundled into them an expectation that the physician will also perform a certain amount of evaluation and management of the patient at the same time. This evaluation and management includes briefly talking to the patient to confirm ongoing symptoms and the treatment plan, any necessary physical exam, and the writing of prescriptions or orders before, during, and after the procedure. Therefore, the entry of a separate *evaluation and management* (E&M) code on the claim is generally not allowed. If it is entered, the coding software will sound an alert, and the software used by the payer will apply an edit to the claim and will not pay the E&M code amount.

However, there are instances in which an E&M code *is* separately payable on the same day as a procedure. For example, say a person is scheduled for a routine screening colonoscopy with biopsy of any abnormal areas seen during the procedure.

---

[82] All coding information in this chapter is taken from CPT 2025 Professional Edition, American Medical Association (2024).

On the day of the colonoscopy, the person calls her gastroenterologist and says that she is having a flare-up of her gastroesophageal reflux disease (GERD) – in other words, she is having bad heartburn. Nevertheless, she still wants to have the colonoscopy that afternoon. The gastroenterologist asks her to come to the office. The person is interviewed and thoroughly examined, and her dose of GERD medication is adjusted. She sees the gastroenterologist at the endoscopy center later that day and undergoes the colonoscopy.

The claim will include the CPT code for colonoscopy with biopsies – 45380. Ordinarily, an E&M code would not be allowed on the claim. However, in this instance, the patient underwent evaluation and management of a completely different problem that is unrelated to the procedure. An E&M code is thus allowed. To indicate that there is an exception to the coding rule, modifier 25 is entered along with CPT 99214 (evaluation and management of an established patient with moderate medical decision-making). Entering this modifier means that the coding software will not create an alert, and the payer will allow the E&M code amount to be paid.

There are several types of conflicts between codes. We will cover these specific conflicts and the edits that deal with them in Chapter 5. For now, I will leave you with the fact that for just one of these types of conflict – the procedure-to-procedure conflict like the example we just saw – there are almost 4.5 million pairs of codes that are not allowed with each other. Remember that there could be more than one of these conflicts on a given claim. The complexity of just one claim can be truly staggering.

Now, another level of complexity comes into the picture. While CPT codes offered standardization of surgical procedures and other medical services in the years after the system was first introduced in 1966, many other procedures, supplies, and services were not covered by a coding system. The items not covered included prosthetic supplies and procedures (think artificial limbs), hearing and vision services, medical and surgical supplies, medications, and many others. In light of this, the federal government introduced in 1978 the "HCFA (Health Care Financing Administration) Common Procedure Coding System" or HCPCS (commonly pronounced hic-picks). After HCFA was replaced by CMS in 2001, HCPCS became the *Healthcare Common Procedure Coding System.*

In 1983, the CPT system was officially made a part of HCPCS and was dubbed HCPCS Level I, with the former HCPCS codes becoming HCPCS Level II.[83] Still, most coding and other healthcare professionals still refer to HCPCS Level I codes as CPT codes, and the AMA continues to release annual *CPT* updates.

---

[83] What is HCPCS?, American Academy of Professional Coders website, accessed June 12, 2025, https://www.aapc.com/resources/what-is-hcpcs

As if having another coding system was not confusing enough, there is some overlap between CPT and HCPCS Level II. For example, CPT code 92557 is used to report a hearing evaluation done at an ear-nose-throat doctor visit. HCPCS II code V5010 is also used to report a hearing evaluation. In Chapter 5, we will see how this overlap can lead to billing errors.

As we finish our look at outpatient claims and physician services, we will explore one last layer of complication. In the last chapter, we saw how inpatient Medicare claims were moved to a prospective payment system in 1983, with many commercial health plans moving to a PPS later. You will recall that the DRG system was implemented as a key part of the IPPS.

You may not find it surprising that there is also an *outpatient PPS* (OPPS).

Outpatient Prospective Payment

By the late 1990s, the IPPS had been up and running for the better part of two decades. Congress authorized HCFA (to become CMS in 2001) to implement OPPS in balanced budget acts passed in 1997 and 1999. The federal system was aimed at all providers of outpatient services for Medicare patients. When OPPS was introduced in August of 2000, it made use of a new structure, the *Ambulatory Payment Classification* or APC.

APCs can be thought of as analogous to DRGs, except they are used for outpatient claims instead of inpatient claims. CPT and HCPCS Level II codes are assigned to APCs and annually updated by CMS. The procedures, services, and supplies assigned to any one APC are considered by CMS to be similar in clinical use and in the amount of work and other resources required. The payment amount for each APC is established by CMS and updated annually. The payment amount is based on cost estimates using national data and geographic wage differences.[84]

Like DRGs for inpatient claims, the APC is not directly determined by the coder. Instead, each CPT and HCPCS code supported by the clinical documentation of a patient encounter is entered into the claim, and the appropriate APC is identified by the coding software. For paper claims, the claims administrator applies the appropriate coding rules to arrive at the proper APC and the associated payment amount.

Another analogy to the IPPS arose for outpatient claims in 2007 when the 3M corporation introduced their *Enhanced Ambulatory Patient Grouping* (EAPG) system. Similar to the run-up to APR-DRGs in the late 1980s, state Medicaid plans had been bemoaning APCs' lack of applicability to the outpatient claims of the pediatric and obstetrical patients in their populations. EAPGs expanded the span of clinical scenarios covered by the OPPS – they were first used for Medicaid patients in New

[84] Teri Guidi, Medicare's Hospital Outpatient Prospective Payment System: OPPS 101 (Part 1 of 2), Journal of Clinical Oncology (2010) 6:6, pp. 321-4.

York. Currently, several state Medicaid plans and a growing number of commercial health plans make use of EAPGs.[85]

We have seen over the past four chapters how the mind-numbingly complicated state of today's medical bill has evolved over not years or even decades but centuries.

We have used the labyrinth as an apt analogy to the maze of rules, regulations, and practices around medical bills. The original labyrinth appears in the ancient Greek myth involving Theseus, who faced in battle the monstrous Minotaur at the center of the labyrinth and defeated him.

We have now set the scene for the next chapter.

Payers are on one side, providers on the other. The plain between is littered with coding guidelines, regulations, this payment system and that one.

The battle is on!

---

[85] District of Columbia Medicaid Outpatient Hospital Payment Method, District of Columbia website, accessed June 12, 2025, https://dhcf.dc.gov/sites/default/files/dc/sites/dhcf/page_content/attachments/DC%20EAPG%20Information%20on%20EAPGs%20Eff%2010-01-2020%20DCO20029.pdf

Chapter 4: Breadcrumbs for the Labyrinth

- Physician payment developed on a track separate from hospital payment, continuing the distinction between professional and facility services that still shapes medical bills.
- CPT gave physicians and payers a standard language for procedures and services, replacing inconsistent written descriptions with codes.
- RBRVS and the Medicare physician fee schedule attempted to tie physician payment to work, practice expense, malpractice cost, and geographic adjustment rather than to arbitrary charges.
- HCPCS incorporated CPT as Level I and added Level II codes for supplies, drugs, durable medical equipment, ambulance services, and other items not fully described by CPT.
- CPT and HCPCS overlap in some areas, which can create confusion and opportunities for inconsistent billing.
- OPPS and APCs became the outpatient counterpart to inpatient DRGs by grouping outpatient services into payment categories.
- EAPGs extended outpatient grouping logic for Medicaid and commercial populations, especially where Medicare's outpatient system did not fit well.

CHAPTER 5
THE INQUEST OF THE CLAIM

It is early 2014, and I am on a flight to Connecticut for a day of meetings. I do not know that this trip is to change the arc of my life.

I had been a fulltime emergency physician until I left clinical practice in 2009 after earning an MBA. I have spent the five years since then working in a company that contracts with hospitals to provide medical chart reviews. On that day in Connecticut, I am to be interviewed for a job in a company that serves health insurance plans. In other words, I am going to the dark side.

I am met at the airport by a kind, funny man who, I guess, is around twenty years older than I am. He drives me to a restaurant where I meet his current boss and thus begins several hours of conversation. By the end of the day, all three of us decide that I would be a good fit for the team.

On the way back to the airport, the man – Dr. Mort Salomon, to whom this book is dedicated – asks me a question.

"Tim, what do you know about DRGs?"

I stammer a little and say, "Well, I know those three letters – D, R, and G. I use them often. Beyond that, I don't know anything."

Mort chuckles. "By this time next year, you will know more about DRGs and medical coding than 99% of physicians in the United States."

I smile and doubt that Mort knows what he is talking about.

A year later, after passing the test to become a certified medical coder, I realize that Mort was right.

When Codes Become Incentives

In the first few years of the 21st century, it was becoming clear that something was not right in the way that medical claims were being paid. Healthcare costs were continuing to rise despite prospective payment systems and other innovations that were meant to control costs. Because of the evolution of employer-based health insurance that we have previously discussed, this rising cost was being borne by employers, who passed on larger and larger portions of the climbing expense to their employees.[86] It was

[86] The Opportunity for Payment Integrity in the US Healthcare Market and Creating the Right to Win, 3one4 Capital website, accessed June 17, 2025,

getting so bad that within a few years Warren Buffett was prompted to call medical costs the "tapeworm of American economic competitiveness"[87], an expense that was sucking the lifeblood out of American businesses and their employees.

One of the problems is illustrated by the story that I told above. There was, and remains today, a disconnect between the clinical practice of medicine and the financial aspects of healthcare. Physicians tend to know very little about how medical claims are coded and submitted. They are largely unaware of the different elements that determine the DRG of an inpatient claim. This disconnect can lead to physicians unintentionally running up the costs of care. However, the misalignment between physicians and those responsible for financing care is only one of the many problems that were coming to light in the first decade of the new millennium.

Through the first five years of the 2000s, hospital consolidation was a growing trend that even today shows no sign of slowing. The merger and acquisition of hospitals and health systems, especially by national for-profit hospital chains, led to higher volumes of billed services with accompanying higher costs. As time went on, this increased volume and cost led to increased scrutiny, both from government regulators and from private sector payer organizations.[88]

As more attention was paid to rising charges from hospitals and other providers, what was found should not be surprising in light of what we have seen about the development of various payment methodologies. Hospitals and providers began using the system against itself.

"Upcoding" is a term that is used to describe the practice of submitting a code that leads to a payment that is higher than the payment of the service that was actually provided. After learning about CPT codes in Chapter 4, you can likely imagine submitting a code whose description is close to the description in the medical record but does not exactly fit, just to get a higher payment. For example, a psychiatrist might enter CPT code 90833 – which should be used to report evaluation and management with 30 minutes of psychotherapy – when in fact the patient was only briefly seen for a medication refill. This very thing happened, resulting in the psychiatrist being fined

---

https://www.3one4capital.com/blogs/the-opportunity-for-payment-integrity-in-the-us-healthcare-market

[87] Chris Arnold, "'Oracle of Omaha': Republican Health Care Bill 'A Huge Tax Cut For Guys Like Me'," National Public Radio website, May 6, 2017, accessed June 17, 2025, https://www.npr.org/sections/thetwo-way/2017/05/06/527193477/the-oracle-of-omaha-condemns-republican-health-care-bill-at-berkshire-meeting#

[88] Hospital Consolidation: Analysis of Acute Sector M&A Activity, Deloitte website (2010) accessed June 17, 2025,
https://www2.deloitte.com/content/dam/Deloitte/us/Documents/life-sciences-health-care/us-chs-hospital-consolidation.pdf

$400,000 and being permanently excluded from receiving Medicare or Medicaid payments.[89]

For the DRG system, upcoding is a little more complicated. You will recall that under the MS-DRG system, payments are higher for claims that report a CC (complicating condition) or MCC (major complicating condition). Hospitals can, therefore, increase their payments simply by adding one of these more highly weighted codes to the claim, without changing the actual intensity of service for the patient. A study done in 2003, looking back at data from the late 80s and early 90s, showed that many hospitals tended to upcode in this fashion in response to changing payment amounts for various DRGs.[90]

The pressure on hospitals and providers in the early 2000s to increase revenue was driven by a few factors. First, as I have already mentioned, there were more and more for-profit entities in the market, organizations that owed it to their shareholders to maximize profits. Also, providers were faced with uncertainty about the payments they would receive, especially from government payers. I can recall, when I was in my emergency medicine practice in the late 1990s, being notified in mid-year that the Georgia Department of Medicaid had already spent their annual budget for the year. Thus, though we were required by federal law to evaluate all patients that came to the ER – including Medicaid patients – we would not be paid for evaluating and treating Medicaid patients until the following year. As Medicare and Medicaid payment rates fell in the 1990s – or disappeared altogether - providers had to make up the difference elsewhere.

Documentation and the CDI Counterweight

Of course, increasing the use of more heavily weighted codes by hospitals and other facilities does not always represent an attempt to "game the system." Because physicians do not always document procedures and services in a way that optimizes a facility's ability to obtain proper reimbursement, these facilities had to devise ways to promote proper documentation.

Though attempting to improve physician documentation was a goal of facilities even under the basic DRG system in place between 1983 and 2007, it was the arrival of MS-DRG in 2007 – with its CCs and MCCs – that provided a renewed impetus. The *Association of Clinical Documentation Improvement Specialists* (ACDIS) was founded in

---

[89] Physician Relationships With Payers, U.S. Department of Health and Human Services, Office of the Inspector General website, accessed June 17, 2025, https://oig.hhs.gov/compliance/physician-education/i-physician-relationships-with-payers/

[90] Leemore Dafny, "How Do Hospitals Respond to Price Changes?" *American Economic Review* (2005) 95(5), pp. 1525-1547.

2007, and it began to provide support for the *clinical documentation improvement* (CDI) specialists that had begun appearing in hospitals over the previous few years.[91]

CDI specialists' main goal is to ensure high quality medical record documentation that supports the codes and other elements that are eventually entered into the claim. For inpatients, they also identify instances in which the inpatient order itself is insufficiently supported. They stalk the nurses' stations on hospital wards, examining charts and waiting to talk to doctors to instruct them on how to better document a certain procedure or diagnosis.

Sometimes, CDI specialists insert a "physician query" into the medical record. This document asks the physician to clarify some notation in the clinical notes of the chart. For example, a query might say:

Dr. Smith,

In the progress note on April 6, you state that the patient has a cough and fever. Does the patient have one of the following diagnoses?

- ☐ *Pneumonia*
- ☐ *Bronchitis, acute*
- ☐ *Upper respiratory infection*
- ☐ *Other*________________

By guiding the physician to more clearly document conditions in the medical record, the CDI specialist helps to ensure that the claim is properly coded and that each code is sufficiently supported.

However, in the mid to late 2000s, companies arose to combat what was felt to be an overreach of the CDI industry as a whole. Payment integrity (PI) companies, like the one that Dr. Salomon hired me to join, serve as a useful counterbalance to the CDI efforts of providers.

For example, a CDI specialist might enter the following query:

Dr. Jones,

In the admitting history and physical, you included "renal failure" in the diagnosis list. Which of the following is correct?

- ☐ *N17.0 Acute kidney failure with tubular necrosis*
- ☐ *N17.1 Acute kidney failure with acute cortical necrosis*
- ☐ *N17.2 Acute kidney failure with medullary necrosis*

This would be considered a "leading query" – not condoned by ACDIS. In this instance, the physician's only option is to select an MCC, since all the listed diagnoses are MCCs.

---

[91] "ACDIS anniversary: Celebrating 15 years of community," *CDI Strategies*, (2022) 16(45), https://acdis.org/articles/acdis-anniversary-celebrating-15-years-community

Through *payment integrity* (PI) activities, performed by payer organizations themselves or by PI vendor companies, codes not supported by the clinical record are challenged and removed. In the above kidney failure example, a DRG validation reviewer – typically a nurse or medical coder with physician oversight – examines the medical record and may discover that there was no clinical or laboratory evidence of tubular necrosis or any of the other serious kidney conditions listed in the physician query. She might find instead that there is evidence of unspecified acute kidney failure (N17.9) which is a CC and thus tends to cause the DRG to pay at a lower rate.

In addition to CDI specialists, PI entities also face the upcoding that sometimes stems from the use of *electronic medical records* (EMRs). EMRs began to appear in hospitals and other healthcare facilities in the late 1980s and early 1990s as the personal computer and internet boom began. [92] The emergency department where I practiced was an early adopter of electronic means of creating clinical notes. We used the original version of Dragon NaturallySpeaking, a second-generation voice-to-text tool, beginning around 1997.

Of course, EMRs do not necessarily lead to upcoding. They are intended to allow easier sharing of important clinical data to the multiple parties that need to have access to that data – primary care physicians, medical and surgical subspecialists, nurses, billing and coding professionals, and anyone else who has legal access and needs the information to provide a service.

However, some of the time-saving features of EMRs can lead to inaccurate coding and billing. For example, most EMRs have built-in macros that allow a physician to easily document a normal physical exam. A physician might click the box for "normal complete physical", and a fully documented complete physical exam auto-populates the chart. This is acceptable if the physician has actually performed all the elements of the exam. However, have you ever had an ER doctor test for sensory versus conductive hearing loss with a tuning fork or all the other obscure observations and tests that might be included in an EMR's complete physical exam? I know that I never have.

In previous versions of the CPT codebook, the degree of completeness of the physical exam was a primary determinant of the proper code used to report office visits, ER visits, and other types of "evaluation and management" (E&M) scenarios. Thus, an incorrectly documented complete physical exam that results from simply clicking the box could lead to choosing an incorrectly high E&M code. Beginning in 2021 and again in 2023, documentation guidelines for E&M codes changed such that there were not specific guidelines for the degree of completeness of the history or physical. Instead, the guidelines focused on the complexity of medical decision making.

---

[92] R. Evans, "Electronic Health Records: Then, Now, and in the Future," *Yearbook of Medical Informatics* (2016), accessed June 17, 2025, https://pmc.ncbi.nlm.nih.gov/articles/PMC5171496/pdf/ymi-11-0s48.pdf

Still, a coder could use documentation of a complete physical exam to support medical decision making of a higher complexity.

As EMRs became more prevalent in offices and hospitals through the first and second decades of the 21st century, reports of improper and even unscrupulous uses of them exploded. In 2012, it was noted that over the decade just ending government payers had been billed at least $11 billion in improper payments, much of it facilitated by EMRs. In 2013, the Center for Public Integrity reviewed more than 50 court cases that involved upcoding, many representing whistleblower lawsuits related to improper EMR uses.[93]

PI firms and payers not only focus on clinical documentation and queries. They also enforce medical coding guidelines and regulations. A key way this is accomplished is by using edits.

Before exploring claims editing, let's talk about the way that medical claims are processed.

From Prior Authorization to Payment

Even before a claim is created, even before a medical service is rendered, the "prior authorization" (prior auth) process is the way by which payers ensure that the planned procedure or other service can proceed. You are likely familiar with the process: 1) you and your doctor agree on a course of action involving a surgical procedure or medication, 2) a form is submitted to your insurance company asking for approval for the medication or surgery, 3) the insurance company either says yes or no, and 4) if no, you and your doctor sometimes can provide additional information and appeal the decision.

In prior auth, medical directors and other personnel within the health insurer organization (or a contracted prior auth vendor) decide about whether the planned medication or procedure is covered by the benefits of the person's policy and whether the planned action abides by the policies of the health insurer.

For example, you and your doctor may decide that you need to have an abdominoplasty operation (a surgery to remove skin and other tissue from your abdominal region). Your best friend had the same operation and was very pleased with the outcome. However, during the prior auth review, it is determined that abdominoplasty is considered by your insurer to be a cosmetic procedure, and your policy does not cover cosmetic surgery.

After prior auth, if required, the service is provided and the claim is prepared by the provider. The claim is submitted, usually electronically in a format called 837 (pronounced eight-thirty-seven), to a clearinghouse and then on to the payer. At this

[93] Cracking the Codes, Reynolds Journalism Institute website, accessed June 17, 2025, https://rjionline.org/rji/wp-content/uploads/sites/2/2020/11/cpi_cracking_the_codes.pdf

point, the first set of edits are applied in a process called *adjudication.* These initial adjudication edits perform such basic tasks as confirming the patient's identity and verifying that the patient is eligible to have a claim submitted on their behalf.

Assuming that the claim passes through the adjudication step, additional edits are usually applied at a stage called *pre-payment claims editing.* Below, we will discuss the various types of edits that have been rolled out over the past 30 years.

The claim and payment amounts are adjusted in response to any edits that "fired", and the payment for the claim – in a format called an 835 – is sent back through the clearinghouse to the provider. Along with the payment is sent an *explanation of benefit* (EOB) – a document that explains what services were paid for and what amount was paid. It also explains the reasons for any denials and lays out the amount that the patient may have to pay. [94]

For commercial plans and Medicare Advantage plans, many of the steps above are provided by third party vendors. It is common to have one entity that serves as the adjudication platform, another entity that is the pre-payment claims editing vendor, and another that serves as the clearinghouse. More than that, there can be more than one vendor in place for pre-payment claims editing. It is common to have a first pass editing vendor along with a second pass and even third pass vendor.

Types of Edits

In the late 1990s, HCFA (later to become CMS) implemented a set of automated medical claims edits it dubbed the *National Correct Coding Initiative* or NCCI. NCCI expanded beyond its initial form to include three types of edits.[95]

First, *procedure-to-procedure (PTP) edits* use tables of procedure codes organized into two columns to identify instances in which two procedures should not be entered on the same claim for the same date of service. For example, CPT code 58953 reports removal of the uterus (hysterectomy) and removal of the ovaries and Fallopian tubes on both sides (bilateral salpingo-oophorectomy), while CPT code 58150 reports a total hysterectomy. These codes should not be reported together because the hysterectomy (58150) is included in (or integral to or inherent in) CPT code 58953. Being paid for both codes would mean being paid twice for the removal of the uterus and being paid

---

[94] The Opportunity for Payment Integrity in the US Healthcare Market and Creating the Right to Win, 3one4 Capital website, accessed June 17, 2025, https://www.3one4capital.com/blogs/the-opportunity-for-payment-integrity-in-the-us-healthcare-market

[95] "Medicare Billing, Commercial System Could Save Hundreds of Millions Annually," United States General Accounting Office website, accessed June 18, 2025, https://www.gao.gov/assets/aimd-98-91.pdf

twice for all the other operating room expenses like nursing staff, routine supplies, anesthesia equipment and supplies, etc.[96]

The second kind of edit – *medically unlikely edits or MUEs* – was added to NCCI 11 years after PTP editing began. MUEs define the maximum numbers of units allowed on a given day for a given patient. Anything more than this maximum number is considered medically unlikely to be correct. An obvious example is CPT code 44950 (appendectomy) that has an MUE of 1. Of course, each of us only has one appendix, thus removing more than one is very unlikely. A less obvious example is CPT 92920 (balloon angioplasty of a coronary artery) which has an MUE of 3. This means that, based on the research of the NCCI team, it is unlikely that any given patient would have more than three arteries in their heart treated with balloon angioplasty in one day.[97]

More recently, CMS introduced *add-on code (AOC) edits.* Add-on codes are CPT codes that are reported in addition to another code. However, these same codes are not allowed if they are reported separate from the primary code. For example, it is allowable to enter CPT add-on code 20932 (implantation of a tendon or cartilage graft) along with primary code 25170 (opening of the wrist joint and repairing it). However, 20932 is removed by the AOC edit if it appears in the absence of the primary code.[98]

Originally intended for fee-for-service Medicare claims, NCCI edits have been adopted by most payers in the U.S. They are widely considered to be standard edits for all types of outpatient claims, regardless of the patient's age or other demographic category. However, non-governmental payers did not stop there. Edits have been developed based on a wide variety of clinical scenarios and payer policies.

Duplicate edits are among the most common edits. They identify claims in which the same code has been entered more than once. Sometimes, this idea of identifying a duplicate code is applied across all the claims for that patient in each timeframe – these are called *frequency edits.* For example, a payer who allows three ultrasounds for an uncomplicated pregnancy might use a frequency edit that will fire when the fourth ultrasound within a 9-month period appears on a claim.

Edits can be used to enforce certain clinical criteria. An example is a payer who has decided that a certain skin substitute product – an artificial skin graft – is not covered because it is deemed to be an experimental treatment. An edit can be created to deny this product when it appears on a claim.

---

[96] "Medicare Billing, Commercial System Could Save Hundreds of Millions Annually," United States General Accounting Office website, accessed June 18, 2025, https://www.gao.gov/assets/aimd-98-91.pdf

[97] "Medicare Billing, Commercial System Could Save Hundreds of Millions Annually," United States General Accounting Office website, accessed June 18, 2025, https://www.gao.gov/assets/aimd-98-91.pdf

[98] Ibid.

Reviewing the Record

Claims editing is not the only way that payers ensure that claims are correct. While claims editing relies on automated algorithms (and increasingly on artificial intelligence), *claims review* is built around teams of reviewers who examine claims data and associated medical records to determine the accuracy of the claim. There are several types of claims review.

Itemized bill review (IBR) is performed on fee-for-service claims (i.e., non-PPS claims). Using established coding rules and payer policies, reviewers look for incorrect line items on the claim. A common error that is found by an IBR reviewer is *unbundling*, in which one line item is integral to the CPT code on another line. For example, an itemized bill may list CPT code 96360 (intravenous infusion, hydration; initial, 31 minutes to 1 hour) and several entries of code 96361 (intravenous infusion, hydration; each additional hour) on a given day for an inpatient who is receiving maintenance IV fluids. The IBR reviewer would recommend removing these CPT codes because maintenance IV fluid services and supplies are bundled in the daily room and board charge for an inpatient.

The way that various diagnosis and procedure codes affect DRG payments has been discussed previously. In *DRG validation reviews*, all the numerous elements of a DRG claim are examined. For example, a claim includes ICD-10 diagnosis code J18.9 (pneumonia) as the principal diagnosis and another diagnosis code K85.90 (pancreatitis) as a secondary diagnosis. This leads to DRG 177 (respiratory infections with an MCC) – because pancreatitis is deemed to be a major complicating condition. The relative weight for this DRG is 1.89, with a paid amount of around $26,000.[99] However, when the DRG validation reviewer examines the medical record, he finds that the admitting doctor wrote, "Possible acute pancreatitis in this patient with confirmed pneumonia. Will get gastroenterology consult." The gastroenterologist's note said, "Doubt acute pancreatitis. The patient has had no abdominal pain, and physical exam is normal. Amylase [blood test to detect pancreatitis] is trending downward. Will follow." On the day of discharge, the admitting physician wrote, "Possible pancreatitis. Patient still without symptoms, and amylase normal. No follow up needed." The DRG validation reviewer rightly concludes that the pancreatitis code is not supported by the medical record, and he removes the code from the claim. This results in the DRG changing to 179 (respiratory infections without a CC or MCC), with a relative weight of 0.93 and a paid amount of around $13,000 – about half as much as the original claim.

---

[99] The PayerPrice website was used to estimate all DRG paid amounts, with payments estimated using 2025 data. https://payerprice.com/rates/177-MS-DRG-fee-schedule

In this DRG validation example, you can see the interaction between CDI professionals on one side, PI professionals on the other side, and physicians in the middle. Let's make some suppositions:

- The hospital in this example had possibly faced lost revenue due to poor physician documentation in the past and had thus launched a CDI initiative.
- CDI specialists trained physicians to document that a diagnosis was "possible" if, after evaluation in the hospital, there is still a possibility that the patient had the condition.
- The hospital coders knew that ICD-10 coding guidelines allow a coder to enter a diagnosis code on the claim, even if the diagnosis is listed as "possible" at the time of discharge.
- On review of the medical record, the DRG validation reviewer saw that, even though pancreatitis was called possible, the condition had been ruled out by the treating and consulting physicians since there were no signs or symptoms of pancreatitis other than one abnormal blood test.
- Just from a logical, practical perspective – does one abnormal blood test that quickly normalizes justify doubling the paid amount for a hospital admission? That does not appear to make sense to me.

The Cost of the Search for Truth

This back-and-forth swing, with payers (governmental and non-governmental) implementing cost containment measures and providers seeking revenue maximization, continues as we race through the third decade of the century – and it has only gotten more complex. There are so many rules around medical coding and the rules change so often that the staffs of payer organizations find it difficult to keep up. Because of this, most health plans and other payer organizations contract with a PI vendor to perform claims editing, claim review, and other PI activities for them.

For hospitals and physician groups, there are analogous organizations, called *revenue cycle management (RCM)* vendors. While CDI professionals help to improve clinical documentation and thus better support claims, RCM firms help providers avoid and respond to denials from payers in addition to assisting with all parts of the provider's revenue cycle – from patient registration and insurance verification all the way through collecting payments for their services.

When I speak to family and friends about the work that I have done in the PI industry, I get lots of questions. Why is all this work necessary? Doesn't everyone know how to submit a claim? Why don't insurance companies just pay without putting up so many barriers?

In response to these kinds of questions, I point to the American legal system. Though our legal system has many faults, I nevertheless consider it to be among the best in the world. Our system of courts and laws has baked into it an adversarial component. Two sides, each with reasons for their beliefs and lawyers to represent them, meet in court to have a [hopefully] impartial judge and jury hear their cases. The intended ultimate outcome – the truth.

I view the medical claim process in a similar way. There are two sides – provider and payer. Each has their representatives - CDI and RCM professionals on the provider side, PI professionals on the payer side. Most of the time, there is no court, judge, or jury – the two sides have to come to an agreement, even if the agreement is to "agree to disagree." However, the majority of my colleagues in the industry have a clear focus on the intended outcome of this work on both sides – the truth. The "integrity" in payment integrity is purposeful. The professional society for CDI specialists, ACDIS, mentioned earlier even changed its name in 2019 to Association of Clinical Documentation *Integrity* Specialists in recognition of its pursuit of the truth.

However, there is a remaining question – Is the work and expense of the existing medical claim system worth the cost? We will tackle this question and explore the financial cost of CDI, PI, RCM, etc. in the last chapter of this book.

Before that – just when you thought it could not get any more complicated…

Chapter 5: Breadcrumbs for the Labyrinth

- More detailed coding made more accurate payment possible, but it also made payment more sensitive to documentation choices and code selection.
- Upcoding can occur when codes are selected to increase payment beyond what the clinical record truly supports.
- Under DRG systems, CCs, MCCs, and severity levels can substantially increase payment, so documentation of comorbid conditions became financially important.
- CDI programs can improve record accuracy, but leading physician queries can push documentation toward higher-paying diagnoses without adequate clinical support.
- Payment integrity programs serve as a payer-side counterbalance by reviewing claims, challenging unsupported codes, and enforcing coding and payment rules.
- Electronic medical records improve access to information but can also amplify inaccurate documentation through copy-forward text, templates, and auto-populated exams.
- Claim edits translate policy and coding rules into software logic, but edits are only as good as the data and rules they use.
- The provider-payer struggle resembles an adversarial search for truth, but the cost of that struggle has become one of the central problems of the system.

CHAPTER 6

THE MAZE'S BRANCHES MULTIPLY

Harold, whom we met in chapter 3, is in a waiting room again.

This time, nothing dramatic is happening. There is no emergency surgery. No one is telling him he needs to stay in bed. No nurse is changing a surgical dressing. Harold is simply seventy-six years old, a little more tired than he used to be, and annoyed that the appointment card in his hand says 9:15 while the clock on the wall says 10:05.

It is the spring of 1994. Harold has had three weeks of shortness of breath and a cough that will not quite go away. His family doctor sends him to the outpatient department of the local hospital for a chest X-ray and some blood work. The doctor also wants a breathing test, but the pulmonary lab cannot fit him in until Thursday. On Friday, Harold returns to his doctor's office to review the results. The doctor changes one inhaler, writes a prescription for an antibiotic, and asks him to come back in a month.

Nothing about this sounds like a complicated episode of care. If Harold were telling the story over coffee, it would take less than a minute.

But the bills tell a different story.

One claim is filed by the hospital outpatient department. Another claim is filed by the radiologist who interpreted the X-ray. A third comes from the laboratory. A fourth comes from the physician's office. The pharmacy transaction does not look like a medical claim at all, even though it is paying for the medicine that is part of the same medical problem. Depending on Harold's insurance coverage, each of these claims may move through a different system, under a different contract, and with different rules for what should be paid.

Harold thinks he had one illness.

The healthcare reimbursement system thinks he had several billable events.

One Encounter, Many Claims

Before we talk about what can be done to simplify, regulate, audit, or otherwise improve the system, we need to spend a little more time with the complexity itself. The prior chapters have looked at the rise of classification systems, the birth of employer-based insurance, the creation of Medicare and Medicaid, and the move toward prospective payment. It would be tempting to think that the introduction of prospective payment systems marked the moment when reimbursement finally became organized. It did not. PPS organized some pieces of the system. Other pieces kept growing in their own directions.

Inpatient hospital claims were only one part of the maze. Outpatient claims, physician claims, ancillary services, durable medical equipment, laboratory claims, ambulance claims, and drug claims all continued to demand their own forms, codes, contracts, and edits. While many payers - principally government payers - moved to prospective payment, many arrangements remained fee-for-service or used some related payment methodology. In these systems, payment still depended heavily on the individual services reported on the claim.

That distinction is important. The type of tension created by PPS is easy to understand. If the payment is fixed in advance, the provider has an incentive to reduce the cost of care. If the documentation on the claim can push the patient into a higher-paying category, the provider also has an incentive to make the illness look more severe. That is the logic we saw with DRGs. Fee-for-service creates a different tension. The payment is not fixed in the same way. Instead, payment generally follows the number and type of services billed. The incentive is therefore not only to describe the patient in a certain way but also to describe the services in a certain way.

In other words, PPS asks, "What kind of case was this?" Fee-for-service asks, "What exactly did you do?"

That second question sounds simple until one tries to answer it in a hospital, an office, or a claims processing system.

The Forms Behind the Maze

Start with the forms.

This may sound old-fashioned because most claims are no longer mailed as paper rectangles with boxes and red ink. Electronic claims are now the ordinary route. Yet, the old paper forms remain useful because they reveal the skeleton underneath the electronic transaction. Billing people still speak in the language of institutional claims and professional claims. Payers still build rules that follow the distinctions those forms created. Auditors still ask whether the line belongs on the facility side or the professional side. The paper may be gone, but the architecture remains.

That architecture is not a small matter. If the wrong kind of claim is used, the wrong rules may apply. If the same encounter is divided into several claim streams, each stream may be individually logical while the combined financial picture looks absurd. A patient can receive a facility bill, a physician bill, a pathology bill, a radiology bill, and a laboratory bill without anyone having lied. The fragmentation is built into the filing system.

A claim form is a map. It tells the payer who the patient is, who provided the care, what diagnoses were treated, what services were rendered, where the services occurred, how much was charged, and how the provider wants to be paid. The map also tells the payer what rules to apply. A hospital claim and a physician claim may describe parts of the same visit, but they do not speak exactly the same language.

The institutional claim form is the CMS-1450, commonly known as the UB-04. CMS describes it as the form an institutional provider can use to bill a Medicare Administrative Contractor when the provider qualifies for a waiver from electronic submission requirements, and CMS notes that it is also used for institutional charges to many Medicaid agencies.[100] That sentence contains several important clues. First, the form pertains to claims from institutions - hospitals, skilled nursing facilities, home health agencies, and other facility-based providers. Second, the paper form survives even though most claims now move electronically. Third, the form is not only a Medicare artifact. Its structure is part of a wider billing culture.

The professional claim form is the CMS-1500. CMS describes this as the standard claim form used by a non-institutional provider or supplier to bill Medicare carriers and durable medical equipment Medicare Administrative Contractors when paper submission is allowed.[101] Physicians, nurse practitioners, physician assistants, therapists, and many other professionals may have services represented on this professional side of the system.

This split echoes the older Blue Cross and Blue Shield distinction. The facility is paid for the room, equipment, supplies, nursing personnel, technical staff, and overhead. The clinician is paid for evaluation, interpretation, procedures, and medical judgment. A patient receives one experience. The system sees at least two sellers.

That is why Harold can sit in one room, have one X-ray, and receive two claims. The hospital outpatient department bills for making the machine, the technologist, the space, and the image available. The radiologist bills for reading the image. If Harold later receives a bill for the blood draw, the laboratory may be billing for the technical performance of the test while his doctor bills for the office visit in which the results are interpreted and a treatment plan is made.

No ordinary patient would design the system this way.

But the system was not designed from scratch. It accreted. Each payer, provider type, claim form, and code set solved a problem that existed at the time. Each solution left behind another layer. Those layers have now hardened into rules, software, contracts, fee schedules, and auditing logic.

---

[100] Centers for Medicare & Medicaid Services, "Institutional Paper Claim Form (CMS-1450)," last modified September 10, 2024, accessed April 24, 2026, https://www.cms.gov/medicare/billing/electronicbillingeditrans/1450.

[101] Centers for Medicare & Medicaid Services, "Professional Paper Claim Form (CMS-1500)," last modified September 10, 2024, accessed April 24, 2026, https://www.cms.gov/medicare/billing/electronicbillingeditrans/1500.

Revenue Codes and Claim Switches

On the institutional side, the UB-04 contains a field that often gets less attention than diagnosis and procedure codes but is essential to understanding facility billing. That field is the revenue code.

A revenue code is a four-digit code used on the institutional claim to identify the general category of accommodation or ancillary service for which the facility is charging. In the CMS-1450 data set, Form Locator 42 is the revenue code field, and the code explains the associated charge reported elsewhere on the claim line.[102] The revenue code does not usually give the full clinical description of the service. Instead, it places the charge into a billing department or service category.

Think of the revenue code as a sign over a doorway. It may tell you that you are entering the laboratory, radiology, pharmacy, emergency department, or operating room area of the hospital's bill. It does not, by itself, tell you precisely what test, image, drug, or procedure occurred. For that, the payer often needs a procedure code, a supply code, a drug code, a unit count, and sometimes a modifier.

This is where the system begins to look less like a form and more like a stack of transparencies. Lay the diagnosis code over the revenue code. Lay the procedure code over that. Add the place of service, type of bill, provider contract, modifier, units, date of service, and payer-specific policy. Now ask whether the line should be paid. The answer may be obvious to a physician who was in the room with the patient. It may be far less obvious to a computer program reading a claim at two o'clock in the morning.

The code set most people associate with medical services is CPT, but CPT is actually part of a larger structure used for claims. HCPCS - the Healthcare Common Procedure Coding System - contains two main subsystems. Level I is CPT, maintained by the American Medical Association, and Level II is a standardized coding system used primarily for products, supplies, and services not included in CPT, such as certain ambulance services, durable medical equipment, prosthetics, orthotics, and supplies.[103]

This is one of those places where a small definition produces a large consequence. If a payer's rules are built around CPT codes, but a service can be represented or supplemented by a HCPCS Level II code, the claim may travel a different path

---

[102] Centers for Medicare & Medicaid Services, Medicare Claims Processing Manual, Pub. 100-04, chap. 25, "Completing and Processing the Form CMS-1450 Data Set," rev. 12423, December 20, 2023, sec. 75.4, accessed April 24, 2026, https://www.cms.gov/Regulations-and-Guidance/Guidance/Manuals/downloads/clm104c25.pdf.

[103] Centers for Medicare & Medicaid Services, "Healthcare Common Procedure Coding System (HCPCS)," last modified April 17, 2026, accessed April 24, 2026, https://www.cms.gov/medicare/coding-billing/healthcare-common-procedure-system.

through the system. It may hit a different edit. It may avoid an edit. It may be paid under a fee schedule instead of bundled into another payment. It may be sent to a different processing unit. The word "code" makes these items sound interchangeable, but they are not.

A code is not only a label. In healthcare payment, a code is a switch. When the switch is flipped, money moves.

This is why claim edits became so important. A claim edit is an automated rule that looks for a condition on a claim and then decides what should happen. The rule may deny a line, suspend the claim for review, request additional information, package one item into another payment, or simply flag the claim for later analysis. A well-designed edit is not merely a denial machine. It is a guardrail. It attempts to keep coding and payment aligned with policy.

The outpatient side of Medicare eventually developed a large editing and payment apparatus of its own. The Integrated Outpatient Code Editor, or I/OCE, edits claims for accuracy, assigns ambulatory payment classifications, assigns status indicators, assigns payment indicators, determines claim disposition based on edits, and makes other payment determinations.[104] It also performs functions that require specific reference to HCPCS codes, modifiers, and ICD-10-CM diagnosis codes.

Notice the words "specific reference." The edit can only apply the rule to the data it receives. A computer cannot compare two codes if one of the codes is missing. It cannot count units of a service if the units are hidden in a place where the edit does not look. It cannot determine whether a service is separately payable if the claim does not present the service in a way the system is built to recognize.

That is not a criticism of computers. It is a reminder that claim data are not the same thing as clinical truth.

The National Correct Coding Initiative, usually shortened to NCCI, is one of the more visible examples of claim editing. CMS developed the NCCI program to promote correct coding of Medicare Part B claims, and its Procedure-to-Procedure edits are intended to prevent improper payment when incorrect code combinations are reported.[105] The same page explains that there is one table of edits for physicians or practitioners and another for outpatient hospital services.

Another kind of edit is the medically unlikely edit, or MUE. CMS describes an MUE as the maximum units of service reported for a HCPCS/CPT code on the vast majority of appropriately reported claims by the same provider or supplier for the

---

[104] Centers for Medicare & Medicaid Services, "Integrated Outpatient Code Editor," last modified February 9, 2026, accessed April 24, 2026, https://www.cms.gov/medicare/coding-billing/outpatient-code-editor.

[105] Centers for Medicare & Medicaid Services, "Medicare National Correct Coding Initiative (NCCI) Edits," last modified March 4, 2026, accessed April 24, 2026, https://www.cms.gov/medicare/coding-billing/national-correct-coding-initiative-ncci-edits.

same beneficiary on the same date of service.[106] The idea is simple. If a claim reports a quantity that is not plausible for a normal encounter, the system should pause before paying it.

A human being can understand the logic immediately. One chest X-ray may be reasonable. Ten identical chest X-rays on the same day for the same patient by the same provider should at least raise a question. A certain number of therapy units may be expected. A number far outside ordinary limits should not sail through payment simply because someone typed it into a field.

But, again, the edit depends on what the claim says. If the service is reported on one line, the units may be obvious. If the same service is split across lines, days, modifiers, revenue codes, or related providers, the logic may be less obvious. If a payer's system does not aggregate the information in the same way CMS does, a pattern that would look suspicious in one environment may look routine in another.

This is where waste and abuse live.

Waste, Abuse, and Workarounds

The phrase "fraud, waste, and abuse" gets repeated so often that the three words can blur together. However, they are different, and the difference lies in the intent. Fraud usually implies intentional deception. Waste may involve unnecessary spending without deliberately intending to lie. Abuse sits in the gray zone: a practice that may not involve a false statement in the most theatrical sense, but that is inconsistent with good medical, fiscal, or business practice. In claims work, the distinction matters legally. In dollars, all three can be expensive.

Most providers are not trying to cheat anyone. Most billing departments are not dens of villains. They are full of overworked people trying to move claims through complicated systems built by other overworked people. Nevertheless, incentives matter. If a system pays more for more lines, more units, more separately identified supplies, more modifiers, or more favorable coding paths, someone will eventually discover the path.

Sometimes the discovery is innocent. A billing employee notices that one way of reporting an item gets denied while another way gets paid. The employee asks a supervisor. The supervisor says, "That is how the payer wants it." The practice becomes routine. No one goes back to ask whether the second way actually describes the service more accurately. Payment success becomes the proof of correctness.

---

[106] Centers for Medicare & Medicaid Services, "Medicare NCCI Medically Unlikely Edits (MUEs)," last modified March 4, 2026, accessed April 24, 2026, https://www.cms.gov/medicare/coding-billing/national-correct-coding-initiative-ncci-edits/medicare-ncci-medically-unlikely-edits-mues.

Other times the discovery is not innocent. A provider or billing vendor may deliberately select codes or claim structures because they know the payer's edits are narrower than the clinical reality. The service has not changed. The patient has not changed. The record may not have changed. Only the billing pathway has changed. Yet the payment may change significantly.

One common vulnerability involves the use of HCPCS codes to move around procedure-code edits. Imagine an edit that is designed to prevent payment for a service when it is included in another, more comprehensive service. If the bundled service is reported with the expected CPT code, the edit fires. If the same resource is instead reported with a different HCPCS Level II supply code, drug code, or miscellaneous code, the edit may not fire unless the payer has deliberately connected those codes in its own logic. CMS explains that HCPCS Level II codes exist for products, supplies, and services not included in CPT, which is precisely why they are necessary - and also why they can create gaps when edits are too narrowly written.[107]

This does not mean HCPCS Level II codes are suspicious. They are essential. A wheelchair, an ambulance service, a prosthetic component, a drug, or a supply may need a code that CPT does not provide. The problem arises when the availability of another code becomes a way to avoid the policy attached to the first code.

This is the core pattern of claims abuse in a complex system: find the rule, then find the path around the rule.

A second vulnerability involves revenue codes. Some payers build edits around procedure codes. That makes sense, because procedure codes are usually the most precise description of the service. But institutional claims also carry revenue codes, and revenue codes are less specific. If a facility submits a revenue code without the expected CPT or HCPCS code, a procedure-code edit may not have its normal trigger. The claim line may still say, in effect, "something happened in this department, and here is the charge," while withholding the more exact description that would allow the payer to test the line against its rules.

A good payer system should catch this. A well-designed outpatient edit should ask whether a given revenue code requires a HCPCS code, whether the bill type permits the combination, whether the service is covered, whether the units are plausible, and whether the charge belongs with another line. But not every payer has Medicare's infrastructure. Not every commercial payer contract demands the same data. Not every legacy system was designed for modern coding detail. In that space, a revenue-code-only line may become a fog bank.

Suppose a hospital outpatient department has a charge that is routinely denied when billed with a particular procedure code because the payer considers it bundled

---

[107] Centers for Medicare & Medicaid Services, "Healthcare Common Procedure Coding System (HCPCS)."

into another service. The compliant answer is to review the policy, review the medical record, correct the coding if it is wrong, appeal if the denial is wrong, and educate the billing staff. The abusive answer is to stop reporting the procedure code and let the charge travel under a more general revenue category. The payer sees a charge. The edit that would have recognized the procedure does not fire. The hospital receives payment it may not have received if the service had been described precisely.

This is not a clever trick. It is a failure of transparency.

It also explains why payers sometimes seem obsessive about missing codes. From the provider's point of view, a denial for a missing code may feel like bureaucratic nitpicking. From the payer's point of view, the missing code may be the difference between a payable service and a hidden duplicate. If the payer cannot see the service clearly, it cannot apply the policy fairly.

That sentence works in both directions. If the provider cannot understand the payer's policy, the provider cannot reliably code the claim. A murky rule invites murky billing.

Consider Harold's breathing test. To Harold, it is one more stop in a week of appointments. To the hospital, it may involve technical staff, equipment, disposable supplies, a facility charge, and perhaps a separate professional interpretation. To the payer, the claim may have a revenue code identifying a service category, a HCPCS or CPT code identifying the test, a modifier identifying a technical or professional component, a diagnosis code supporting medical necessity, and units of service. If any one of these pieces is missing, mismatched, or intentionally chosen to avoid an edit, the payment answer changes.

Now multiply Harold by millions of patients.

CMS notes that insurers process billions of claims each year, and that standardized coding systems are essential for orderly and consistent claims processing.[108] That statement sounds dry, but it is the entire reason the coding machinery exists. A nation cannot adjudicate billions of medical claims by having a nurse, a physician, an accountant, and a lawyer sit around a table to discuss each one. The system has to use codes. It has to use forms. It has to use algorithms. It has to use edits.

Because it uses those things, it can be gamed through those things.

There is a cruel symmetry here. The more detailed the code system becomes, the better it can represent real clinical and billing differences. But the more detailed it becomes, the more opportunities it creates for strategic selection. A single vague code is too blunt to be fair. A thousand precise codes are difficult to police. The system chooses precision and then spends decades trying to control what precision makes possible.

---

[108] Centers for Medicare & Medicaid Services, "Healthcare Common Procedure Coding System (HCPCS)."

This is why the word "abuse" in billing can feel so slippery. A provider may argue that it followed the available code descriptors. A payer may argue that the selected code defeats the intent of the policy. The provider may point to the medical record. The payer may point to the edit table. The provider may point to past payments. The payer may point to a manual. The patient, if he is unlucky enough to be drawn into the dispute, may wonder why anyone needs this many words to explain one breathing test.

The answer is that healthcare payment is not only paying for care. It is paying for care as represented through data.

Once that is understood, the forms make more sense. The CMS-1450 is not merely a bill. It is a structured institutional data set. The CMS-1500 is not merely a physician invoice. It is a professional data set. Revenue codes are not merely accounting labels. They are routing devices. HCPCS codes are not merely descriptions. They are payment triggers. Edits are not merely denials. They are policy translated into software.

Every one of these tools can be used properly.

Every one of them can also be misused.

When Complexity Becomes Culture

This is not unique to Medicare. Medicare is often the easiest system to discuss because it publishes rules, manuals, code editor logic, and educational materials. Commercial payers may use Medicare as a starting point, but many add their own contracts, fee schedules, proprietary edits, prior authorization rules, medical policies, and payment exceptions. Medicaid agencies may use state-specific systems. Self-funded employer plans may rent a network from one company, use a third-party administrator from another, and apply a reference-based pricing rule from a consultant. The patient's card may carry one logo while the payment decision is influenced by three organizations the patient has never heard of.

This is why a claim that pays under one plan may deny under another even when the patient, provider, and service are the same. One payer's edit table includes the code combination. Another payer's does not. One requires a procedure code with the revenue code. Another allows a broader revenue line. One follows Medicare's NCCI edits closely. Another modifies them. One updates quarterly. Another updates late. One bundles a supply. Another pays it separately. None of this is visible to the patient.

It may not even be visible to the clinician.

Clinicians often say they do not want to think about billing. This is understandable. They did not go to medical school to study form locators. But the claim is now the financial shadow of the medical record. If the medical record does not clearly describe what was done and why, the billing office fills in the gaps. If the payer cannot understand the claim, the payer denies or pays incorrectly. If the provider learns which claims pay and which do not without understanding why, the billing system trains itself toward payment rather than accuracy.

That is how complexity becomes culture.

And once complexity becomes culture, reform becomes harder.

A simple rule such as "do not bill separately for items that are included in another service" sounds easy until someone asks what counts as included. Is the supply included? Is the drug included? Is the technical component included? Is the professional interpretation included? Is the service included only when performed on the same day? What if a modifier indicates a distinct service? What if the patient moved from the emergency department to observation? What if the provider is in a hospital-based clinic that looks like an office but bills as part of the hospital?

Each answer becomes another rule.

Each rule becomes another edit.

Each edit becomes another opportunity to route around it.

This is why the claim form discussion belongs before any serious discussion of solutions. Without understanding the claim, one cannot understand the problem. Waste and abuse do not always appear as a giant false diagnosis or a completely fictional patient. Often they appear as a small shift in how a real service is represented. A supply becomes a separately payable item. A bundled service becomes a new line. A line that should carry a procedure code carries only a revenue code. A modifier that should mean "distinct" becomes a password. A miscellaneous code becomes a drawer into which inconvenient items are placed.

The system responds by adding edits.

The edits respond by creating denials.

The denials respond by creating workarounds.

The workarounds respond by creating more edits.

At some point, everyone is tired.

The patient is tired of bills he cannot read. The physician is tired of queries about documentation. The hospital is tired of denials. The payer is tired of appeals. The coder is tired of ambiguous notes. The auditor is tired of being told that every questionable pattern is just the way the software works. The software vendor is tired of being blamed for rules it did not write. And somewhere in the middle of all of this, the original clinical question - what happened to the patient, and what should it fairly cost? - becomes harder to see.

This does not mean forms, codes, and edits are bad. The opposite is true. Without them, the system would be chaos. The problem is that the tools built to manage complexity have become complex enough to need their own tools. Then those tools create incentives of their own.

The institutional claim form exists for good reasons. The professional claim form exists for good reasons. Revenue codes exist for good reasons. HCPCS codes exist for good reasons. NCCI edits and MUEs exist for good reasons. The I/OCE exists for good reasons. But good reasons do not make a system immune from bad use.

In fact, the better a system gets at paying from data, the more valuable it becomes to control the data.

That is the uncomfortable point at the center of this chapter.

The modern reimbursement system is not merely complicated because bureaucrats enjoy complication, though it is sometimes hard to avoid that suspicion. It is complicated because it is trying to convert a messy human event into standardized payment. The patient speaks in symptoms. The clinician speaks in diagnoses and treatment plans. The facility speaks in departments, supplies, and charges. The payer speaks in policies, contracts, and edits. The claim is the translation device among them.

Translations can be faithful.

They can also be manipulated.

So when we ask what can be done, we should resist the easy answer that the system merely needs fewer codes or fewer forms. Fewer codes can mean less accuracy. Fewer edits can mean more improper payment. More edits can mean more administrative burden. More documentation can mean less time for care. Less documentation can mean more ambiguity. Every proposed simplification moves pressure somewhere else.

Still, the fact that a problem is hard is not an excuse for leaving it alone. A system that depends on precise claim data must require precise claim data. A payer that denies claims based on policy must write policies that providers can understand. A provider that wants payment must describe services honestly and completely. A regulator that demands compliance must recognize when rules are so convoluted that ordinary compliance becomes unrealistic.

Those are not solutions yet. They are conditions for solutions.

For now, the point is simply this: the complexity did not end with DRGs. It spread outward through forms, revenue codes, HCPCS codes, edits, modifiers, and payer contracts. PPS changed one battlefield. Fee-for-service and hybrid payment systems left many others in place.

Harold's week of outpatient care is not unusual. That is what makes it useful. The ordinary encounter is where the system reveals itself. A patient sees a doctor, has a test, fills a prescription, and waits to feel better. Behind him, claims begin to multiply. Each claim asks to be translated. Each translation can be accurate, mistaken, incomplete, or strategic.

The next question is whether the people responsible for the system have the will to make honest translation easier than manipulation.

That is the question we finally turn to next.

Chapter 6: Breadcrumbs for the Labyrinth

- Prospective payment did not replace fee-for-service reimbursement; it grew alongside it.
- Institutional and professional claims use different forms because American healthcare payment still separates facility and professional services.
- The CMS-1450, or UB-04, is the institutional claim form; the CMS-1500 is the professional claim form.
- Revenue codes categorize facility charges but usually do not provide the full clinical description of the service.
- HCPCS includes CPT codes as Level I and other supplies, products, and services as Level II.
- Claim edits such as NCCI Procedure-to-Procedure edits and Medically Unlikely Edits are policy rules translated into software.
- When a claim omits or changes the code an edit expects, the intended safeguard may not work.
- Submitting a revenue code without the expected CPT or HCPCS code can obscure the exact service and may allow a claim line to avoid procedure-code edits.
- Not every workaround is fraud, but every workaround that hides the true service undermines the integrity of payment.
- Any serious solution must make accurate billing easier than strategic ambiguity.

CHAPTER 7
THE BILL ARRIVES AT THE KITCHEN TABLE

The envelope is thin, which seems unfair.

Maria stands at the kitchen counter with a letter opener in one hand and a cup of reheated coffee in the other. Her husband has already gone to work. Their youngest child has left a cereal bowl in the sink. The dog is nosing at the trash can. Nothing about the room suggests danger.

The danger is in the envelope.

Three weeks earlier, Maria had taken her son to an urgent care center for a fever, sore throat, and a rash that worried her enough that she did not want to wait until Monday. The clinician swabbed his throat, looked in his ears, checked the rash, and gave instructions that turned out to be exactly right. By Tuesday he was back at school. The illness had ended.

The paperwork had not.

The first notice came from the health plan and said in bold letters that it was not a bill. The second notice came from the urgent care center and very much was a bill. The third came through a patient portal that Maria rarely uses and showed a balance different from the balance on the paper bill. A fourth message, a text sent at 8:06 on a Saturday morning, offered a payment plan and warned that unpaid balances could be sent to collections.

Maria lines the papers on the counter. The EOB says the total charge was $612. The amount allowed by the plan was $186. The plan paid $0 because the family had not yet met the deductible. The provider bill asks for $231. The portal asks for $186. The text message gives no details at all.

Her son is healthy. Maria is angry.

The Last Translation

Most of this book has been about the machinery that sits behind the medical bill: disease classification, procedure codes, prospective payment, professional claims, facility claims, edits, denials, chart reviews, revenue cycle management, and payment integrity. Those things may seem remote from the ordinary patient. They are not.

The patient bill is the last translation. The clinical event becomes documentation. Documentation becomes codes. Codes become claim lines. Claim lines pass through edits, contracts, deductibles, coinsurance, copayments, denials, adjustments, appeals, and payments. At the end of that long path, a balance appears on a statement or in a portal.

That balance may be correct. It may be partly correct. It may be wrong. The patient usually has no easy way to know.

This is one reason the current system feels so unfair. A patient is asked to behave like a careful consumer, but the bill she receives is not written like a normal consumer invoice. It is the visible surface of a transaction that has already passed through layers the patient never saw.

Imagine buying groceries in such a system. You pick up milk, apples, bread, and chicken. Three weeks later, your grocery plan sends a letter saying it is not a bill. The store sends a bill showing the full shelf price, a negotiated price, a food-network adjustment, a household deductible, and your share. The bakery sends a separate bill because the bread was baked by a different professional group. The butcher sends a portal message because the chicken involved a professional interpretation. You call customer service and are told the store is in network, but the person who sliced the bread was not.

No one would tolerate that at a grocery store. In healthcare, it happens every day.

This Is Not a Bill

The document that most often starts the confusion is the *explanation of benefits* (EOB). An EOB is supposed to explain how a claim was processed. It usually lists the provider, the date of service, the billed charge, the allowed amount, the portion paid by the plan, and the amount the patient may owe.

Notice the words 'may owe'. The health plan usually does not know whether the patient has already paid part of the bill. The health plan may not know whether another payer is involved. The health plan may not know whether the provider will write off part of the balance, apply a prompt-pay discount, or correct the claim later. The EOB is therefore not the same thing as the provider's bill.

This distinction is logical inside the system and maddening outside it.

Patients are often told to wait for the bill before paying. Then the provider bill arrives, and it may not match the EOB. Sometimes the difference is innocent. The provider may have sent the statement before the claim finished processing. A secondary insurance plan may still be pending. The portal balance may lag behind the paper statement. A contractual adjustment may not have posted yet. Sometimes the difference is not innocent. The provider may be billing for a balance that should have been adjusted away. The claim may have been denied because the wrong code was submitted. The patient may be getting charged for a service that should have been bundled into another payment.

To the patient, all of these explanations sound like the same sentence: the bill is confusing.

The Math of Patient Responsibility

The patient balance on a medical bill generally comes from a handful of concepts, each simple in isolation and bewildering in combination. The billed charge is the provider's starting price. The allowed amount is the amount the payer's rules or contract recognize for the service. The contractual adjustment is the amount the provider agrees not to collect because of the payer contract. The deductible is the amount the patient must pay before the plan begins paying certain benefits. A copayment is a fixed dollar amount. Coinsurance is a percentage of an allowed amount. The out-of-pocket maximum is supposed to limit the patient's annual spending for covered services, subject to the plan's rules.

That last phrase can lead to a lot of expense: subject to the plan's rules.

A service that is not covered may not count toward the out-of-pocket maximum. An out-of-network service may have a separate deductible or may not be covered at all. A drug may be covered under the pharmacy benefit but not the medical benefit, or the other way around. A hospital may be in network while a physician group billing separately is not. A preventive service may be free in one setting but not in another because a diagnosis code or modifier changes how the claim is treated.

This is why patients can do everything they were told to do and still receive a bill they did not expect. The patient hears, 'Your insurance covers this.' The system means, 'This service may be covered if the provider is in the right network, the claim is coded correctly, the diagnosis supports medical necessity, the service is not excluded by the plan, the deductible has been met, any required prior authorization was obtained, and no other policy exception applies.'

Those two sentences are not the same.

One Visit, Many Bills

A common source of patient anger is the discovery that one encounter can produce many bills. An emergency room visit is the classic example. The patient may receive a facility bill from the hospital, a professional bill from the emergency physician group, a radiology bill if imaging was interpreted, a pathology bill if tissue or lab work was reviewed, an ambulance bill if transportation was involved, and perhaps a separate bill from an out-of-network clinician who never introduced himself as a separate business entity.

From the patient's point of view, she went to the hospital. From the payment system's point of view, she consumed services from several different legal, clinical, and billing entities.

The system is not always wrong to separate these entities. The hospital owns the building, staffs the nursing units, buys the equipment, keeps the lights on, and maintains the emergency department. The physician group supplies professional judgment. The radiologist interprets the image. The pathologist interprets the specimen. The ambulance service may be owned by a municipality, a private company, or the hospital. Each entity has real costs and real workers.

But the patient does not experience the encounter as a collection of vendors. She experiences it as care.

This mismatch is one of the deepest reasons medical bills feel untrustworthy. The clinical experience is unified, while the billing experience is fragmented. The patient remembers one night. The mailbox remembers six claim numbers.

Surprise Bills and the Limits of Protection

The most notorious version of fragmented billing is the surprise out-of-network bill. Congress addressed part of this problem through the *No Surprises Act* (NSA), which created federal protections for many emergency services and for certain non-emergency services provided by out-of-network clinicians at in-network facilities. The law also created an *independent dispute resolution* (IDR) process for certain payment disputes between providers and plans.

The protections matter. A patient should not be financially punished because an emergency physician, anesthesiologist, radiologist, or other hospital-based professional turned out to be outside the network even though the patient went to an in-network hospital. Nor should an unconscious patient be expected to shop for network status while being wheeled down a hallway.

Yet the law did not make medical bills simple. It did not erase deductibles. It did not make every provider in network. It did not cover every type of service. It did not remove disputes between providers and payers. It merely moved some of those disputes away from the patient. That is real progress, but it is not the end of the maze.

A good reform often works that way. It closes one corridor and leaves others open. The patient is safer than before, but still not free from confusion.

Collections and the Fear Factor

Medical debt has a different emotional weight than ordinary consumer debt. A person who buys a television on credit understands that a purchase was made and a price was accepted. A person who receives a medical bill may have been sick, frightened, sedated, in pain, or focused on a child or spouse. The price may not have been knowable in advance. The final bill may arrive months later. By then, the patient may not remember every test, supply, or clinician involved.

When such a bill is followed by collection notices, the tone changes from confusion to fear. A patient who does not understand the bill may pay simply to make the fear stop. This is not proof that the bill was valid. It is proof that fear is a powerful collection tool.

Hospitals and other providers do need to collect legitimate patient responsibility. No system can function if every balance is treated as optional. But collection practices should be tied to clarity. If a provider cannot explain why a balance is owed, which claim produced it, how the payer processed it, whether financial assistance applies, and whether the amount reflects the payer contract, then the provider should not rush the account toward collections.

The moral order should be simple: explain first, collect second.

Charity Care and the Hidden Door

Another source of frustration is that many patients do not know when help is available. Nonprofit hospitals often have financial assistance or charity care policies. Some for-profit hospitals and physician groups also offer discounts, payment plans, or hardship programs. These policies may be posted online, mentioned in small print, or explained only after the patient asks the right question.

A financial assistance policy is only as humane as the process required to use it. If the application is difficult to find, requires documents the patient cannot easily provide, or is offered only after threatening statements have been sent, the policy may exist more on paper than in practice.

Patients should not have to know magic words to receive help. A billing system that can identify payer contracts, deductible status, denial codes, and patient balances should also be able to identify when a person may qualify for financial assistance and say so plainly.

A Practical Reading of the Bill

Even in an unreformed system, patients are not helpless. A patient reviewing a bill should first match it to the EOB. The provider name, date of service, and patient responsibility should line up. If the bill arrives before the EOB, waiting may be wise unless the provider gives a clear reason not to wait. The patient should ask whether all insurance has been applied, whether the provider is billing the allowed amount rather than the billed charge, whether any denial is being appealed, and whether financial assistance is available.

Patients should also ask for an itemized bill when the total is large or confusing. Itemization does not magically make a bill correct, but it provides the detail needed to ask better questions. It can reveal duplicate charges, supplies that seem implausible, professional charges mixed with facility charges, or services that were cancelled but still billed.

The goal is not to turn every patient into a coder, auditor, and contract analyst. That would be absurd. The goal is to give the patient enough visibility to challenge obvious errors and enough confidence not to pay merely because a letter looks official.

The Patient as the Last Auditor

There is something perverse about making the patient the last auditor of the claim. By the time the bill reaches the kitchen table, the claim may have passed through provider billing staff, clearinghouses, payer adjudication systems, edits, reviews, denials, appeals, adjustments, and payment posting. If all those systems still produce a balance that cannot be explained, the patient should not be blamed for being confused.

And yet patients often discover errors no machine found. They know they did not receive a brace. They know the appointment was cancelled. They know the doctor never came into the room. They know the insurance card was given at registration. They know the bill is for the wrong child. Their knowledge is not technical, but it is real.

A better system would honor that knowledge. It would make patient questions easy to submit and easy to resolve. It would not force a person to call three phone numbers and repeat the same story. It would not require the patient to mediate between a provider and a payer who disagree about a code. It would not convert confusion into collections.

The American medical bill is not only a financial document. It is a trust document. Every unexplained balance weakens trust. Every corrected error strengthens it. Every clear EOB, honest bill, prompt adjustment, and fair payment plan tells the patient that the system may be complicated, but it is not indifferent.

That is the standard we should demand.

Chapter 7: Breadcrumbs for the Labyrinth

- The patient bill is the final translation of the clinical event, documentation, coding, adjudication, contract rules, and payment decisions.
- An EOB is not a bill; it explains claim processing, but it may not reflect payments already made, secondary coverage, later corrections, or provider billing decisions.
- Patient responsibility can include deductibles, copayments, coinsurance, noncovered services, out-of-network balances, or amounts created by claim errors.
- One clinical encounter can generate multiple bills.
- The No Surprises Act protects patients from many surprise out-of-network bills, but it does not make all medical billing simple.
- Collections should follow clear explanation, not substitute for it.
- Financial assistance policies should be easy to find, easy to understand, and offered before patients are pushed toward collections.
- Patients should not be expected to become coding experts, but they should be given enough information to identify obvious errors and ask useful questions.

CHAPTER 8
THE CONTRACT BEHIND THE CLAIM

Keyanna Jones thought she had done the difficult part before her daughter ever put on the hospital gown.

Her daughter, Chloë, was in kindergarten and had been born with ptosis, a drooping eyelid that could eventually interfere with her sight. The recommended surgery was not experimental, exotic, or mysterious. It was a known procedure, performed by a specialist, with billing codes that could be typed into a letter and read back by an insurance representative.

The problem was geography. Near the Jones family's home in Wentzville, Missouri, Keyanna could not find a pediatric ophthalmologist who both handled Chloë's condition and took the family's insurance. The closest in-network specialist was hundreds of miles away. So, Keyanna asked the insurer for an exception: treat this out-of-network doctor as if he were in network because the network did not really offer a practical option.

The insurer agreed. A letter arrived saying the family had permission to use the doctor because there was not an available provider in the area. The letter listed billing codes and said the services would be covered at the network level. A second letter approved the surgery. To a parent, those words sounded like the same promise in two envelopes: you may go, and the plan will handle it as in-network.

On surgery day, Chloë understood the medicine and the mask better than most adults understand an insurance contract. A hospital worker had given her a coloring book that explained the steps. The anesthetic smelled like bubble gum. The surgery went well. She ate popsicles afterward and went home healing as everyone hoped she would.

Then the real operation began, the one no one had drawn for her in a coloring book.

The bill totaled $15,188. The insurer initially paid $1,775.79. That left the family owing $13,412.21. The operation had not changed. The child had not changed. The diagnosis had not changed. The billing codes had not turned into different codes after the fact. What changed was the path the claim took through the contract.

Keyanna called, appealed, uploaded letters, and tried to explain that she had received approval. She was told there was no record of approval for the surgery as in-network. She was also told, in effect, that the contractual issues between the insurer and the doctor and hospital would not allow the claim to be paid differently.[109]

---

[109] Cara Anthony, "An Insurer Agreed To Cover Her Surgery. A Politician's Nudge Got the Bills Paid," KFF Health News, Aug. 26, 2025.

A Code Is Not a Price

The chapters before this one have spent a great deal of time on codes. That is necessary because codes describe the service for payment purposes. But a code is not a price. A CPT code may identify an office visit. A HCPCS code may identify a drug. A DRG may group an inpatient stay. A revenue code may identify a facility department. None of these, by itself, tells you what a particular payer will pay a particular provider for a particular patient on a particular day.

The payment answer comes from the code plus the contract plus the plan design plus the patient's status in the plan year plus the payer's policy plus the provider's billing behavior. This is why price transparency is so hard. The system can publish charges. It can publish negotiated rates. It can produce estimates. But the final patient responsibility may still depend on facts that are not known until the claim is processed.

A code opens the door. The contract decides which room you enter.

Networks and the Promise of Discount

A provider network is, at its most basic level, a list of providers that have agreed to a payer's terms. The payer wants predictable access and predictable prices. The provider wants patient volume and reliable payment. The patient is told to stay in network because the plan has negotiated better terms there.

This arrangement can work well. Network contracts can protect patients from full billed charges. They can define timely filing rules, appeal rights, covered services, documentation expectations, and payment amounts. They can bring order to a system that would otherwise be a wild market of charges.

But networks also create a new source of confusion. A hospital may be in network while a physician group inside the hospital is not. A laboratory used by an in-network doctor's office may be out of network. A plan may lease another network in one state and use its own network in another. A provider directory may be out of date. A patient may choose an in-network facility only to discover that one part of the encounter took a different contractual path.

The word 'network' sounds like a fence. In practice, it is more like a web. It has strong strands and loose strands, and patients often do not know which strand they are standing on until the bill arrives.

The Chargemaster and the Shadow Price

Hospitals maintain lists of charges for items and services. These lists are often called *chargemasters*. The chargemaster is sometimes treated in public discussion as the villain of the story, and there is reason for that. Chargemaster prices can be far higher than the amounts most insured patients' plans actually allow. They can look arbitrary. They can make a simple service appear terrifyingly expensive.

Still, the chargemaster is not the whole story. For many insured patients, the billed charge is a starting point rather than the final price. A payer contract may pay a percentage of charges, a fixed fee schedule amount, a case rate, a per diem, a DRG amount, an APC amount, or a carved-out amount for a specific implant, drug, or high-cost supply. The contractual adjustment may erase much of the billed charge before patient responsibility is calculated.

That does not mean the billed charge is harmless. If a patient is uninsured, out of network, treated by a provider without a contract, or caught in a plan design that uses charges in some way, the chargemaster can matter a great deal. It also matters because many payment methods still use charges somewhere in the calculation. A price that looks imaginary can still cast a real shadow.

The Menu of Payment Methods

Provider contracts contain many payment methods. A fee schedule pays a set amount for each code. A percent-of-charge contract pays a percentage of the billed charge. A per diem pays a set amount per day. A case rate pays a set amount for an episode or procedure. A DRG pays based on the inpatient grouping. An APC pays based on outpatient grouping. A capitation arrangement pays a set amount per member per month, whether or not the member uses services. A shared savings arrangement may reward providers who keep total costs below a target while meeting quality measures.

Each method carries incentives. Fee schedules reward volume and code selection. Percent-of-charge arrangements can reward higher charges. Per diems can reward longer stays unless other controls exist. Case rates and DRGs reward efficiency but may create pressure to discharge earlier or code more precisely. Capitation rewards prevention and efficiency but can create concern about underuse. Shared savings rewards coordination but depends on measurement that can itself become complex.

There is no payment method free of incentive. The question is whether the incentive points toward better care, honest documentation, and fair payment - or toward manipulation.

Carve-Outs, Stop-Loss, and the Exception Factory

Even a contract that begins simply can become complicated quickly. A payer and hospital may agree to pay routine outpatient surgery through a fee schedule but carve out expensive implants. They may pay inpatient stays by DRG but add a stop-loss provision when charges exceed a certain threshold. They may pay separately for new technology, high-cost drugs, blood products, organ acquisition costs, or trauma services. They may treat emergency care differently from elective care. They may have special rules for observation stays, rehabilitation, skilled nursing, or readmissions.

These exceptions often have reasonable origins. A hospital does not want to lose enormous amounts on an unusually expensive implant. A payer does not want to pay every supply line separately when it should be included in a surgical payment. Both sides know that outlier cases exist. Both sides build exceptions.

The trouble is that exceptions become another maze. Billing staff must know them. Payer systems must adjudicate them. Auditors must test them. Patients may be affected by them. A claim that seems straightforward clinically may become complicated financially because one line crosses a contract threshold.

The Employer Behind the Card

Many Americans receive health coverage through an employer. The insurance card may carry the logo of a large national health insurance company, but the financial risk may belong to the employer rather than to the insurance company. In a fully insured plan, the employer generally pays premiums and the insurer bears the claim risk. In a self-funded plan, the employer pays the claims, often using an insurer or administrator to run the network, process claims, and provide customer service.

This distinction matters. A self-funded employer may make plan-design decisions that shape deductibles, exclusions, prior authorization requirements, pharmacy coverage, and vendor relationships. The health plan name on the card may not be the entity ultimately paying the bill.

The federal law that governs many employer benefit plans is the *Employee Retirement Income Security Act* (ERISA). A self-funded employer plan may also rely on a *third-party administrator* (TPA) to perform administrative functions. To the patient, none of this is obvious. She sees a card. Behind the card may stand an employer, an administrator, a network, a pharmacy benefit manager, a stop-loss insurer, a care management vendor, and several claims editing systems.

The card is simple because it has to fit in a wallet. The arrangement behind it may fill a filing cabinet.

Reference Prices and Narrow Doors

Some employers and plans have tried to control costs through reference-based pricing or narrow networks. In a reference-based pricing arrangement, a plan may set payment as a percentage of Medicare or another benchmark rather than using a traditional negotiated contract. In a narrow network, the plan limits in-network access to selected providers willing to meet price, quality, or contractual requirements.

These approaches can lower costs, but they can also confuse patients if not explained clearly. A patient may believe a service is covered, only to learn that the plan will pay only a reference amount and the provider may seek more. A narrow network may offer lower premiums but fewer choices. The trade-off may be reasonable, but it must be visible.

Hidden trade-offs breed resentment. Clear trade-offs allow consent.

Transparency and Its Frustrations

In recent years, federal rules have pushed hospitals and plans to disclose more pricing information. Hospitals must post standard charge information, including machine-readable data and consumer-friendly information for certain shoppable services. The *machine-readable file* (MRF) is meant for computers to read, compare, and analyze. Plans have also faced transparency requirements intended to make negotiated rates and cost-sharing information more available.

Transparency is necessary. It is not sufficient.

A spreadsheet containing thousands or millions of rates may be technically transparent and practically useless to a patient. A negotiated rate may not reveal the final patient responsibility. A shoppable service may become non-shoppable when complications occur. An estimate may be accurate for the main procedure but miss anesthesia, pathology, imaging, drugs, implants, or facility fees. A website may exist but be too difficult to navigate. A price may be published but not comparable because hospitals describe service packages differently.

The point is not that transparency rules are bad. They are important steps. But transparency that merely dumps data into public view is not the same as understanding. A flashlight is useful only if someone points it where people are walking.

Why the Same Care Has Different Prices

Patients often ask why the same service costs different amounts for different people. The answer is that American healthcare prices are not one price. They are a stack of prices. There is a billed charge. There may be a cash price. There may be many negotiated rates, one for each payer contract. There may be Medicare rates, Medicaid rates, workers' compensation rates, auto insurance rates, and self-pay discounts. There may be bundled prices, carve-outs, and outlier provisions. There may be different amounts for the same service depending on site of service.

This is not a normal market price. It is a negotiated administrative outcome.

The system developed this way because each payer solved its own problem. Medicare needed national payment systems. Medicaid programs needed state-specific methods. Employers needed networks. Commercial insurers needed contracts. Hospitals needed revenue. Physicians needed fee schedules. Vendors built tools to manage the differences. Each solution made sense to someone at the time. Together they became the contract labyrinth.

The Contract as a Moral Document

A contract may seem like a dry business instrument, but in healthcare it is also a moral document. It determines which providers are available, which services are paid, how disputes are resolved, how quickly claims must be filed, how denials are explained, how much patients may owe, and whether unusual cases are handled with flexibility or rigidity.

Contracts can support integrity. They can require complete claim data, clear payment rules, prompt correction of errors, fair appeal processes, and patient protections. They can also reward ambiguity, hide important terms, create incentives for upcoding, or shift confusion to the patient.

When a patient receives a bill, she is not only seeing the result of a clinical encounter. She is seeing the result of a contract she never negotiated and may never read.

That fact should make everyone involved a little more humble. Payers should write clearer policies. Providers should bill according to the contract rather than the most profitable interpretation of the contract. Employers should understand the plans they buy or fund. Vendors should not profit from preventable confusion. Regulators should recognize that transparency must be usable, not merely available.

A code without a contract is incomplete. A contract without clarity is dangerous. A bill without both is a riddle.

Chapter 8: Breadcrumbs for the Labyrinth

- A medical code identifies a service, but the contract and plan rules determine much of the payment.
- Provider networks can lower patient costs and organize access, but they also create confusion.
- Chargemaster prices are often starting points rather than final prices.
- Contracts may use fee schedules, percent-of-charge payments, per diems, case rates, DRGs, APCs, capitation, shared savings, carve-outs, and stop-loss provisions.
- Employer coverage may be fully insured or self-funded.
- ERISA, TPAs, reference-based pricing, and narrow networks are part of the hidden structure behind many insurance cards.
- Price transparency is necessary, but machine-readable data and posted rates do not automatically create understandable patient prices.
- Healthcare contracts are moral documents because their terms shape access, payment, disputes, patient balances, and trust.

CHAPTER 9
THE OTHER LABYRINTH: DRUGS, DEVICES, AND SPECIALTY CARE

The medicine is smaller than a dime and costs more than the refrigerator in the kitchen.

James is standing at the pharmacy counter, looking through the clear plastic bag at a bottle containing thirty tablets. The pharmacist has already tried the insurance card twice. The second attempt took longer, which James had learned is sometimes a good sign. This time it was not.

The plan wants prior authorization.

James calls his doctor's office from the parking lot. The nurse says they sent the form yesterday. The pharmacy says it has not gone through. The plan says the request is pending. The manufacturer's coupon website says he may be eligible, except that the rules depend on the type of insurance. The doctor's office has samples, but only enough for two weeks.

The illness is in his body. The maze is in his phone.

When the Claim Is a Pill

Most of the earlier chapters have focused on hospitals, physicians, facility claims, professional claims, and the codes used to describe medical services. But a major part of modern healthcare spending now flows through drugs, devices, biologics, durable medical equipment, and specialty care. These items have their own code sets, their own contracts, their own intermediaries, and their own forms of confusion.

For many patients, this is the part of the system they meet most often. They may not be hospitalized for years. They may rarely see a specialist. But they stand at the pharmacy counter every month. They refill insulin, inhalers, anticoagulants, cancer drugs, migraine medications, immune suppressants, and heart medicines. They learn whether the plan prefers one drug over another, whether the deductible applies, whether a coupon helps, whether the pharmacy is preferred, and whether the drug must come from a specialty pharmacy.

A prescription seems like it should be simpler than a hospital bill. One doctor writes one prescription. One pharmacy fills one bottle.

It is not that simple.

The Pharmacy Benefit and the Medical Benefit

One of the first twists is that drugs may be paid under different benefits. A pill picked up at the pharmacy is commonly processed under the pharmacy benefit. A drug infused in a physician office or hospital outpatient department may be processed under the medical benefit. The same disease may therefore produce very different billing pathways depending on how the medication is administered.

Think of two patients with inflammatory bowel disease. One takes an oral medication from a pharmacy. Another receives an intravenous biologic infusion in an outpatient department. The first claim may travel through the pharmacy system. The second may travel through the medical claims system, carrying HCPCS drug codes, revenue codes, administration codes, units, and possibly facility and professional charges.

The drug may be the center of care in both cases. The payment systems may barely resemble each other.

This distinction matters to patients because deductibles, coinsurance, prior authorization, site-of-care rules, copayment assistance, and appeals may differ by benefit. A patient may be told that a drug is covered, only to learn that it is covered under one benefit and not the other, or covered in one site but not another.

PBMs and the Middle of the Middle

A central figure in the drug labyrinth is the *pharmacy benefit manager* (PBM). PBMs generally work with health plans, employers, pharmacies, and drug manufacturers to administer pharmacy benefits. They may create or manage formularies, negotiate rebates, operate pharmacy networks, process prescription claims, run mail-order or specialty pharmacies, and apply rules such as prior authorization and step therapy.

The PBM sits in the middle of a market that already has many middles. The manufacturer sets a list price. The wholesaler distributes the drug. The pharmacy dispenses it. The plan or employer pays part of the cost. The patient pays a copay, coinsurance, deductible amount, or sometimes a cash price. Rebates and fees may move after the point of sale. The price the patient sees at the counter may not reveal the money moving behind the counter.

This is where public debate becomes heated. PBMs argue that they negotiate lower net costs and help plans manage drug spending. Critics argue that rebate structures, spread pricing, vertical integration, and preferred pharmacy arrangements can distort incentives and make patient costs higher or less understandable. Both points can be true in different circumstances. A middleman can create value. A middleman can also collect value while obscuring who is paying whom.

The patient at the counter usually does not care which theory wins. She wants to know whether she can afford the drug today.

Formularies, Tiers, and Step Therapy

A formulary is a plan's list of covered drugs. The formulary may sort drugs into tiers. A low tier may carry a small copayment. A preferred brand tier may cost more. A nonpreferred brand or specialty tier may cost much more. Some drugs may require prior authorization. Some may require step therapy, meaning the patient must try one or more preferred drugs before the plan covers the requested drug. Some may have quantity limits.

These tools are not automatically unreasonable. A plan should be able to prefer a safe, effective, lower-cost drug over a more expensive alternative when the clinical result is likely to be the same. A plan should be able to prevent unsafe quantities or duplicative therapy. Without management, drug spending can become unsustainable.

But management becomes harmful when it is opaque, slow, or too rigid. A patient who has already failed a preferred drug should not be forced to fail it again because the documentation is missing. A patient stable on a medication should not be switched casually because a rebate arrangement changed. A patient with cancer, autoimmune disease, or epilepsy may not have the luxury of administrative delay.

A formulary should guide care. It should not become a wall that only the persistent can climb.

NDCs, J-Codes, and the Problem of Drug Identity

Drugs need identifiers just as diagnoses and procedures do. The *national drug code* (NDC) identifies drug products in a way that reflects the labeler, product, and package. Medical claims for physician-administered drugs often use HCPCS Level II codes, including many J-codes. A single HCPCS code may correspond to multiple NDCs, package sizes, manufacturers, or biosimilar products, depending on the drug and coding rules.

This creates a familiar translation problem. The clinician thinks about the medication. The pharmacy thinks about the dispensed product. The manufacturer thinks about the package. The payer thinks about the covered code, units, policy, and price. The medical claim may need both a HCPCS code and NDC information. If the wrong units are reported, payment may be wrong. If a drug is billed under a miscellaneous code because a specific code has not yet been assigned, review becomes harder. If a biosimilar has a different code or modifier requirement, the claim may travel a different payment path.

Again, the code is not only a label. It is a switch.

ASP, AWP, and the Price That Is Not the Price

Drug pricing has its own vocabulary. Medicare Part B drugs are commonly tied to *average sales price* (ASP) methodology. Older commercial arrangements or references may use *average wholesale price* (AWP), a benchmark that has often been criticized because it may not represent an actual transaction price. Pharmacy claims may involve list prices, negotiated rates, rebates, dispensing fees, ingredient cost formulas, maximum allowable cost lists, and patient cost-sharing rules.

The result is that the price of a drug depends on which price one means. There is the list price that may appear in public discussion. There is the net price after rebates. There is the amount paid to the pharmacy. There is the amount the plan recognizes. There is the amount the patient owes at the counter. There is the amount a manufacturer coupon may cover. There is the amount a government program may prohibit a coupon from covering.

A patient can reasonably ask, 'What does this drug cost?' The system may answer, 'To whom?'

Buy and Bill

Many physician-administered drugs are handled through a process often called buy and bill. The physician practice, clinic, or hospital buys the drug, stores it, administers it, and then bills the payer for both the drug and the administration service. This model can make sense for infusions, injections, chemotherapy, and biologics that require clinical supervision.

It also carries financial risk. The provider may purchase an expensive drug before knowing whether the claim will be paid. The payer may worry that the site of care is more expensive than necessary. The patient may face coinsurance based on a high allowed amount. Specialty pharmacies may be inserted into the process through white bagging or brown bagging arrangements, in which the drug is shipped to the provider or patient rather than purchased directly by the administering facility.

Each model has safety, cost, and logistics concerns. A hospital may argue that it needs control over drug sourcing and storage to protect patients. A payer may argue that specialty pharmacy distribution reduces cost. A patient may wonder why a medicine prescribed by her doctor cannot simply arrive where it is needed, when it is needed, without a fight among entities she did not choose.

Specialty Pharmacies and Narrow Channels

Specialty drugs often require special handling, monitoring, education, or adherence support. Plans may require these drugs to be filled through specialty pharmacies. Sometimes those pharmacies are owned by or affiliated with the same corporate family as the PBM or insurer. This vertical integration can create efficiencies, but it can also raise concerns about steering, competition, and transparency.

For the patient, specialty pharmacy can feel like both help and obstacle. The specialty pharmacy may call to coordinate delivery, provide nursing support, manage refills, and check side effects. It may also require long phone calls, repeated benefit verification, temperature-controlled shipping, signatures, copay assistance enrollment, and separate prior authorizations.

A local pharmacist who knows the patient may be removed from the process. The medication may be delayed because a shipment missed a signature. The doctor may not know whether the drug arrived. The patient may become the messenger among doctor, plan, PBM, specialty pharmacy, and manufacturer assistance program.

That is not patient-centered care. That is patient-centered administration.

Devices, DME, and the Objects of Care

Drugs are not the only products that produce billing complexity. Wheelchairs, walkers, oxygen equipment, hospital beds, glucose monitors, braces, prosthetics, wound care supplies, and sleep apnea devices all bring their own rules. Many of these items fall under *durable medical equipment* (DME) or related supply categories. They may require prescriptions, documentation of medical necessity, rental-versus-purchase determinations, supplier enrollment rules, modifiers, replacement schedules, and proof that the patient still needs the item.

Once again, the logic is not absurd. A payer should not buy unlimited equipment without evidence that it is needed. A supplier should document what was delivered. A patient should not receive unsafe or unnecessary devices. But the administrative burden can be heavy. A patient with severe lung disease may care less about whether oxygen is billed as rental or purchase than about whether oxygen arrives before bedtime.

The device may be simple. The documentation may not be.

Biosimilars and the Meaning of Similar

Biologic drugs and biosimilars add another layer. A biosimilar is not a traditional generic in the way patients often understand that word. It is highly similar to an already approved biologic product, with no clinically meaningful differences in safety, purity, and potency under the applicable regulatory standard. Biosimilars can create competition and lower costs, but adoption may be affected by payer formulary decisions, physician comfort, patient concerns, interchangeability rules, coding, reimbursement, and rebate arrangements.

The patient hears that a cheaper alternative exists. Then she learns that cheaper to the system may not mean cheaper to her, that the plan may prefer one product this year and another next year, or that the infusion center's payment differs depending on the code and contract. The word 'similar' becomes financially complicated.

The Same Pattern Again

The drug and device world may seem separate from DRGs, CPTs, APCs, and claim edits, but the pattern is familiar. A real clinical need must be translated into a payment system. The translation requires codes. The codes interact with contracts. The contracts create incentives. The incentives create workarounds. The workarounds require edits, reviews, audits, appeals, and more rules.

The patient experiences the result as delay, cost, or confusion. The doctor experiences it as paperwork. The pharmacist experiences it as a rejected claim. The plan experiences it as utilization management. The employer experiences it as trend. The manufacturer experiences it as market access. The PBM experiences it as formulary management. Each party may be telling the truth from its own position. The system becomes incomprehensible because every truth is partial.

This is why reform cannot focus only on hospital bills. A patient who can understand an inpatient claim but cannot obtain an affordable medication is still trapped in the labyrinth. A payer that cleans up facility edits but leaves drug rebates opaque has not solved the problem. A provider that documents a diagnosis perfectly but cannot help the patient navigate a specialty pharmacy has not completed the work of care.

Healthcare payment is no longer only about paying for visits and admissions. It is about financing molecules, devices, data, logistics, and long-term management of chronic disease.

Toward Honest Drug Payment

A better drug and device payment system would not pretend that every expensive therapy should be covered without question. Some products are unsafe, ineffective, experimental, duplicative, or overpriced. Payers need tools to manage use. Employers need affordability. Patients need protection from financial ruin. Providers need reliable pathways for clinically appropriate therapy.

The standard should be the same one we have used elsewhere: honest translation. The prescription should translate into a coverage answer that is timely and understandable. The drug code should identify the product accurately. The unit count should match what was given. The rebate or discount structure should not make the patient pay more because the list price is artificially high. The site of care rule should be based on safety and value, not merely leverage. The appeal process should be fast when delay threatens health.

No one should have to become an expert in formularies, NDCs, PBMs, ASP files, specialty pharmacy shipping rules, and manufacturer coupons to take a medicine prescribed by a doctor.

Yet that is where many patients find themselves.

The other labyrinth is not beside the first one. It is connected to it. The path that began with a medieval physician accepting an honorarium now runs through codes for molecules, contracts for rebates, portals for prior authorization, and delivery tracking for biologics packed in ice.

The maze has changed shape. The need for a thread has not.

Chapter 9: Breadcrumbs for the Labyrinth

- Prescription drugs, biologics, devices, DME, and specialty care have their own payment pathways and can be confusing.
- A drug may be processed under the pharmacy benefit or the medical benefit, and the benefit used can change coverage, cost-sharing, authorization, and appeals.
- PBMs administer many pharmacy benefits.
- Formularies, tiers, prior authorization, step therapy, and quantity limits can control costs but can also delay or obstruct needed care when applied poorly.
- Drug identity may involve NDCs, HCPCS J-codes, units, package sizes, biosimilars, and miscellaneous codes.
- Drug prices may refer to list price, net price, ASP, AWP, negotiated pharmacy payment, patient cost-sharing, or manufacturer assistance.
- Buy-and-bill arrangements and specialty pharmacy distribution shift financial risk, logistics, and control among providers, payers, pharmacies, and patients.

CHAPTER 10
THE WALL AROUND HEALTHCARE

Denise has learned the hold music by heart.

She is sitting in the parking lot of the oncology center with her phone pressed to her ear and a paper cup of coffee going cold in the console beside her. The morning started with hope. Her doctor had looked at the scan, pointed to the computer screen, and said that the new medicine offered a reasonable next step. Not a miracle. Not a promise. A reasonable next step. In cancer care, that phrase can feel like a rope thrown across a river.

Then the nurse said the treatment could not start today.

The health plan wanted prior authorization.

Denise had heard the phrase before. Her husband had needed it for an MRI. Her neighbor had needed it for a diabetes medication. She had always understood it vaguely, the way most of us understand the parts of a car engine we never intend to touch. It meant permission. It meant paperwork. It meant waiting.

Now it means something else. It means that the drug that is sitting somewhere in the building, mixed by a pharmacist or waiting in a refrigerator, is not yet a treatment. It is a possibility.

The nurse is kind. She explains that the request has already been sent, that the chart notes were attached, that the plan may respond today or tomorrow, and that if it denies the request the doctor can appeal. Denise nods because nodding is easier than asking the question she wants to ask.

How can the answer be no when the cancer is yes?

Across town, the request has entered a queue. A portal has received data. A code has been recognized. A policy has been matched. A nurse may review the file. A medical director may be asked to decide whether the requested drug is medically necessary under the plan's rules. A vendor may be involved. An algorithm may have sorted the case into a bucket. A clock has started running.

Denise hears only the hold music.

Before the Claim Exists

In Chapter 5, we briefly encountered prior authorization as one stop on the road from treatment to payment. That mention was not enough. Prior authorization deserves its own chapter because it is different from most of the billing machinery we have discussed. A claim review asks whether a service that already happened should be paid. Prior authorization asks whether the service should happen with the plan's financial blessing in the first place.

That difference matters. A post-payment audit can frustrate a hospital. A denied claim can injure a physician practice. A confusing bill can frighten a patient at the kitchen table. But prior authorization can stand between the patient and the treatment itself. It is not merely an accounting process. It is a coverage decision made in the narrow and anxious space between diagnosis and care.

The official name is *prior authorization* (PA). Many clinicians call it prior auth. Some patients call it permission. Some doctors call it interference. Some payers call it utilization management. All of those descriptions contain a piece of the truth.

At its best, PA is a guardrail. It can prevent unsafe care, duplicative care, inappropriate settings, premature surgery, expensive treatments that are not supported by evidence, and the use of a high-cost therapy when an equally good lower-cost alternative is available. A plan that pays for everything without question is not being generous with its own money. It is spending premiums, employer dollars, tax dollars, and eventually patient wages.

At its worst, PA is a tollbooth built in front of a clinic door. It can delay necessary care, force patients to repeat failed treatments, cause appointments to be canceled at the last minute, shift hours of unpaid work onto physician offices, and make sick people prove the obvious to strangers while their symptoms continue.

Both realities exist. That is why the subject is so hard. A serious discussion of PA cannot begin with the assumption that every request should be approved. It also cannot begin with the assumption that every denial is a brave act of stewardship. The question is not whether health plans should ever ask questions before paying. The question is whether the questions are necessary, timely, transparent, clinically sound, and humane.

How a Service Becomes an Authorization Request

The process usually begins in the ordinary flow of care. A physician recommends an MRI, a surgery, a home health visit, a sleep study, a wheelchair, a biologic infusion, a specialty drug, a rehabilitation stay, or a hospital admission. The patient thinks of the recommendation as a medical plan. The provider's billing staff thinks of it as a set of codes, dates, diagnosis links, benefit categories, and documentation requirements. The health plan thinks of it as a request to commit money under a contract.

The provider first has to know whether PA is required. That sounds simple. It is not. The answer may depend on the patient's plan, the service, the diagnosis, the place of service, the provider's network status, the patient's age, the requested drug dose, the number of units, the body part being imaged, the number of therapy visits already used, and whether the same service was recently authorized by a different plan.

One insurer may require PA for a lumbar spine MRI only after conservative therapy has failed. Another may require it for nearly all advanced imaging. A third may waive it for certain providers. A fourth may require it only when the service is performed in a hospital outpatient department rather than a freestanding imaging center. The patient sees one test. The plan sees a decision tree.

The provider then submits the request. In a modern setting, the request may go through a payer portal, an electronic health record connection, a phone call, a fax, a pharmacy system, or a third-party vendor platform. Some requests are still submitted in ways that would have looked familiar in the 1990s: forms, faxes, phone calls, copied records, and staff members writing the same information in different boxes because each plan asks for it differently.

The data may include patient identifiers, the ordering provider, the rendering provider, the requested service code, the diagnosis code, the place of service, the requested date or date range, the amount or number of units, and clinical notes. If the service is a drug, the request may also include the drug name, dose, route, frequency, prior medications tried and failed, laboratory results, and whether the drug is being requested under the pharmacy benefit or the medical benefit.

The first review is often mechanical. Is the patient enrolled? Is the plan active? Is the provider in network? Is the service covered by the benefit? Is the request complete? Is a PA required at all? Has another authorization already been granted? Is the requested date outside the allowed window? Is the code valid? Is the diagnosis one that can support the service?

Many requests die temporarily at this stage, not because a doctor or nurse decided the service was wrong, but because a box was empty or a document was missing. A missing office note, a wrong date of birth, a transposed identification number, a diagnosis code that does not match the policy, or a request sent to the wrong vendor can turn a medically reasonable plan into an administrative delay.

The patient rarely sees this part. The patient sees a canceled appointment.

Utilization Management and Medical Necessity

The broader system is called *utilization management* (UM). That phrase is not used at kitchen tables, but it is used constantly inside health plans. UM is the set of processes by which a payer tries to make sure that healthcare services are appropriate, necessary, efficient, and covered. PA is one UM tool. Concurrent review of an ongoing hospital stay is another. Retrospective review after services are delivered is another.

A related phrase is *utilization review* (UR). In everyday speech, UM and UR are sometimes used almost interchangeably. If we are being precise, UM is the larger management function, while UR often refers to the act of reviewing a particular service, admission, or continued stay against criteria. The distinction is not important to most patients. It is important to the people who build the workflows.

Inside a health plan, the PA request is usually measured against medical necessity criteria. Those criteria may come from the plan's own coverage policy, Medicare rules, Medicaid rules, a commercial evidence-based guideline product, a pharmacy and therapeutics committee, a specialty society guideline, a contract provision, or a combination of these sources. In some areas, especially Medicare Advantage, the plan must also consider whether the service would be covered under traditional Medicare rules. The rules are not always as clear as either side wishes.

Consider knee replacement surgery. A patient may have severe arthritis. The surgeon may believe that replacement is appropriate. The plan policy may require documentation of X-ray findings, duration of pain, functional limitation, failed conservative therapy, physical therapy, use of anti-inflammatory medication unless contraindicated, and body mass index or smoking status considerations. The patient hears, "You need a new knee." The plan asks, "Does the record prove that this new knee meets our policy today?"

That difference between clinical judgment and documented policy compliance is one of the central tensions of PA. Physicians often think in terms of the patient in front of them. Plans have to think in terms of consistent rules across thousands or millions of patients. A good policy should leave room for individual judgment. A good physician should understand that an insurer cannot pay for every preference as if it were a necessity. The trouble begins when the policy becomes a substitute for judgment or when judgment refuses to explain itself in a way the policy can recognize.

The Health Plan Work Queue

Once the request is received, it enters a work queue. Some requests are auto-approved because the service is low risk, the documentation is complete, the requesting provider has a strong approval history, or the rules are simple. Some are auto-routed to staff because they involve high cost, unusual diagnoses, conflicting information, missing documentation, out-of-network care, or services known to vary widely in use.

A non-clinical intake worker may check for completeness. A nurse reviewer may compare the record to criteria. A pharmacist may review a drug request. A physical therapist may review rehabilitation services. A medical director may be asked to decide a case that cannot be approved by the reviewer. In many organizations, the first-line reviewer can approve a request that meets criteria but cannot deny one that fails criteria. A denial often requires review by a physician or other clinician with authority under the plan's rules.

That design is meant to protect patients. It recognizes that denying care is different from approving it. Still, the protection works only if the reviewer has adequate information, enough time, appropriate expertise, clear policy, and independence from improper pressure. A rushed physician reviewer applying a vague policy to an incomplete chart can reach a technically defensible answer that is still wrong for the patient.

Sometimes a vendor performs the review. Radiology benefits managers may review advanced imaging. Pharmacy benefit managers may handle drug authorizations. Behavioral health vendors may manage mental health or substance use services. Post-acute vendors may review skilled nursing facility stays, home health, or rehabilitation. The patient may think her insurance company denied the request. In practical terms, a subcontractor may have made the decision according to delegated authority and plan policy.

Vendor delegation can bring specialized expertise. It can also splinter accountability. A physician office may call the plan and be told to call the vendor. The vendor may say the plan controls the benefit. The plan may say the vendor controls the criteria. The patient may be told that no one can speak to her because the request came from the provider. Everyone has a role. No one feels like the door.

Timeframes and the Cruelty of Waiting

Health plans do not have unlimited time to decide. Rules vary by line of business and jurisdiction, but timeframes generally distinguish between standard requests and urgent or expedited requests. In the 2024 CMS Interoperability and Prior Authorization final rule, CMS required impacted payers, excluding certain marketplace issuers, to send prior authorization decisions within 72 hours for expedited requests and seven calendar days for standard requests, with additional requirements around denial reasons, public metrics, and electronic data exchange for medical items and services rather than drugs.[110]

Those timeframes are an improvement. They are also, from the patient's perspective, strangely elastic. Seventy-two hours can be medically tolerable for some requests and frightening for others. Seven days can be a minor inconvenience if the question is a non-urgent imaging test. It can be devastating if the delay means another week of pain, another missed paycheck, another day without mobility equipment, or another round of cancer treatment rescheduled.

The clock itself can become contested. Did the clock start when the request was submitted, or when the plan received all required documentation? Was the request

---

[110] Centers for Medicare and Medicaid Services, "CMS Interoperability and Prior Authorization Final Rule CMS-0057-F," January 17, 2024, accessed online; the rule requires impacted payers to improve prior authorization processes, including certain API requirements, decision timeframes, denial reasons, and public metrics.

urgent under the plan's definition, or merely urgent in the patient's life? Did the provider submit the request to the correct place? Did the plan ask for more information, pausing or restarting the process? Did the patient know any of this was happening?

Administrative time and human time are not the same. Administrative time is measured in business days, turnaround requirements, queue status, and pending information. Human time is measured in pain, fear, missed work, disease progression, family worry, and the number of times a person checks the phone.

This is one of the reasons PA creates such resentment. The plan may be following the rule. The reviewer may be working diligently. The provider may have submitted the required records. Yet the patient experiences the whole thing as abandonment. She was told what she needs, and now everyone is explaining why she cannot have it yet.

Pharmacy Prior Authorization

Pharmacy PA has its own rhythm. A patient presents a prescription at the pharmacy. The pharmacy submits the claim electronically. The response comes back: prior authorization required. The pharmacist tells the patient that the doctor must contact the insurance company. The patient calls the doctor. The doctor's staff may not know there is a problem until that call. The staff then sends a request, often through an electronic prescribing platform or a payer portal. The plan or PBM asks why the requested drug is needed.

The questions may be reasonable. Has the patient tried the preferred generic drug? Is the diagnosis one for which the drug is approved or supported by evidence? Is the dose within recommended ranges? Is the requested quantity appropriate? Is there a safer alternative? Is the drug being prescribed by the right kind of specialist? Are required labs documented?

The questions may also be maddening. The plan may ask whether the patient tried a medication that is contraindicated. It may ask for a lab value already in the record. It may require failure of a drug the patient failed years ago under a different plan. It may approve a medication for six months even though the condition is chronic and lifelong. It may reject a continuation request because the prior authorization expired on a date no one remembered.

Step therapy is especially painful to patients who have already walked the steps. A plan may require that a patient try Drug A before Drug B because Drug A is cheaper and works for many people. There is nothing inherently wrong with that idea. It becomes wrong when the patient has already failed Drug A, cannot safely take Drug A, or is stable on Drug B and is forced to risk deterioration because the new plan wants the old ritual repeated.

For chronic disease patients, PA can become seasonal weather. Every year, or every plan change, or every drug renewal, the storm returns. Rheumatoid arthritis, inflammatory bowel disease, multiple sclerosis, migraine, psoriasis, diabetes, asthma, cancer, and mental health conditions can all involve medications that are expensive, highly managed, or both. The patient may not fear the needle, the infusion chair, or the pill. The patient fears the gap.

Medical Prior Authorization

Medical PA looks different. It may involve imaging, surgery, inpatient admission, outpatient procedures, durable medical equipment, home health, therapy visits, genetic testing, radiation therapy, sleep studies, or site-of-care rules. The request may be submitted days or weeks before a scheduled service. Sometimes the patient never knows the authorization exists unless something goes wrong.

An imaging example is common. A patient with back pain sees a physician. The physician orders an MRI. The plan policy may require red-flag symptoms, neurologic deficits, cancer history, infection signs, trauma, or a period of conservative therapy. The plan is trying to prevent unnecessary imaging. That is not unreasonable. Many cases of back pain improve without MRI, and imaging can lead to incidental findings, anxiety, and unnecessary procedures.

Yet an individual patient does not live inside a population curve. If she is the patient whose weakness is getting worse, whose pain keeps her from working, or whose cancer history makes the symptom different, a denial based on a generic pathway can feel like the system is proving its prudence on her spine.

Surgical PA brings a different set of problems. A surgeon may schedule an operation only after office visits, imaging, tests, and discussions. The hospital reserves operating room time. The patient arranges transportation, childcare, leave from work, and help at home. Then the authorization is still pending the day before surgery. The clinical problem may be old. The administrative decision is new. The patient may have built a week of life around a door that has not opened.

Post-acute care is another important area. After a hospitalization, a patient may need a skilled nursing facility, inpatient rehabilitation, home health, or durable medical equipment. The discharge planner sends records. The plan reviews whether the level of care is medically necessary. The hospital wants to discharge the patient safely. The patient wants to leave the hospital but fears going home without help. The family is told that a decision is pending.

Here, PA affects not only the patient but the flow of the entire hospital. A patient waiting for authorization may occupy a bed needed by another patient in the emergency department. A denial may send the family scrambling for a different facility or a different plan. An approval that comes late on a Friday afternoon may be useless if the receiving facility cannot admit until Monday. Administrative timing becomes capacity management.

The Peer-to-Peer Ritual

When a request does not meet criteria, the provider may be offered a *peer-to-peer* discussion. The phrase suggests collegial medical conversation: one physician speaking with another physician about the patient. Sometimes that is what happens. The ordering doctor explains the clinical nuance. The plan reviewer clarifies the missing information. The request is approved. The system works.

Other times, the peer-to-peer feels like theater. The clinician on the plan side may not practice in the same specialty. The time slots may be inconvenient. The call may be limited to information already in the record. The reviewer may be allowed to overturn the decision, or may merely document the conversation. The ordering physician may be squeezed between patient visits, trying to persuade a stranger while running behind in clinic.

The AMA's 2024 prior authorization survey reported that only a small share of physicians believed peer-to-peer conversations often or always involved a peer with appropriate qualifications. The same survey reported that 94 percent of physicians said PA always, often, or sometimes delayed necessary care, 78 percent said it often or sometimes led patients to abandon a recommended treatment, and physicians and their staff spent an average of 12 hours per week completing prior authorizations.[111]

Those numbers should not be treated as neutral measurement in the way a laboratory value is neutral. The AMA represents physicians and has a clear advocacy position. Still, the findings align with what almost any physician office can tell you from daily experience: PA consumes time, creates friction, and often stands between the medical plan and the patient.

The peer-to-peer should be reserved for cases in which actual medical judgment can change the outcome. It should not be a toll paid in physician hours before the plan will read the record carefully. If the plan needs a specific lab value, ask for it. If the policy requires a failed medication trial, say so. If the denial is because the requested site of care is not preferred, say that. Forcing a doctor to call another doctor just to learn what the denial letter should have said is waste dressed up as dialogue.

---

[111] Tanya Albert Henry, "Exhausted by prior auth, many patients abandon care: AMA survey," American Medical Association, July 18, 2024, accessed online. The AMA reported physician survey results including delays in care, patient abandonment of treatment, serious adverse events, weekly practice workload, and burnout related to prior authorization.

Denials, Appeals, and the Second Maze

A denial is not always the end. Most plans have appeal processes. Medicare Advantage, Medicaid managed care, commercial plans, and employer plans all have rules around internal appeals, external review, urgent appeals, and notices. The exact process varies. That variation is part of the problem.

A good denial notice should tell the patient and provider what was denied, why it was denied, what policy or criterion was used, what information was missing if any, how to appeal, how quickly an appeal must be filed, whether expedited review is available, and whether the patient has the right to external review. A bad denial notice gives a vague medical necessity statement and leaves everyone guessing.

Appeals reveal an uncomfortable truth. In Medicare Advantage, KFF reported that plans denied 3.4 million prior authorization requests in whole or in part in 2022, about 7.4 percent of 46.2 million requests. Only about one in ten denied requests was appealed, yet 83.2 percent of appealed denials were overturned.[112]

The high reversal rate does not prove that every initial denial was wrong. Appeals tend to be selective. Providers and patients are more likely to appeal cases they believe they can win or cases that matter enough to fight. Still, the combination of low appeal rates and high reversal rates should make us uneasy. It suggests that many patients may accept no for an answer not because the no is correct, but because the path to challenge it is too steep.

This is where real people disappear in the statistics. A denial that is overturned after two weeks may count as a successful appeal. For the patient, it may have meant two weeks without medication. For the family, two weeks of phone calls. For the physician office, two weeks of staff time. For the employer, two weeks of impaired work. For the hospital, two weeks of delayed discharge planning. For the health plan, it may show up as a corrected decision. For the patient, it was a wound.

The HHS Office of Inspector General has raised similar concerns in Medicare Advantage. In a 2022 report, OIG found that some prior authorization requests denied by selected Medicare Advantage organizations met Medicare coverage rules, raising concerns that beneficiaries could be delayed or prevented from receiving medically necessary care.[113]

The correct response is not to abolish every review. The correct response is to make the first answer better and the second answer easier.

---

[112] KFF, "Medicare Advantage Plans Denied a Larger Share of Prior Authorization Requests in 2022 Than in Prior Years," August 8, 2024, accessed online.

[113] U.S. Department of Health and Human Services, Office of Inspector General, "Some Medicare Advantage Organization Denials of Prior Authorization Requests Raise Concerns About Beneficiary Access to Medically Necessary Care," April 2022, accessed online.

Why Plans Use Prior Authorization

To understand PA honestly, we need to say something that patients and physicians may not want to hear: health plans use PA because the healthcare system gives them reasons to use it. There is overuse in medicine. There is low-value care. There are inappropriate settings of care. There are drugs prescribed before safer or cheaper alternatives are tried. There are hospitals that would rather use their own expensive outpatient departments than lower-cost community sites. There are vendors and manufacturers with strong financial incentives to expand use of their products. There are providers who practice aggressively because they believe more care is better care, and providers who practice aggressively because more care pays better.

A payer responsible for millions of people cannot ignore these realities. If a plan pays for every high-cost request without review, premiums rise. Employers pay more. Workers pay more. Taxpayers pay more. Patients with deductibles and coinsurance pay more. Money spent on low-value care is not available for primary care, mental health, rural hospitals, nurses, or new therapies that really do change lives.

A plan also has a safety argument. Some requested services are not merely expensive; they are risky. Surgery carries complications. Imaging can lead to downstream procedures. Opioids, sedatives, certain cancer drugs, biologics, and many other medications have serious potential harms. A requirement for documentation can protect patients from casual escalation.

That is the best version of PA: evidence-based stewardship of shared resources and patient safety.

The problem is that a tool built for stewardship can be used for delay. A plan can save money by discouraging use, by making requests difficult, by requiring repeated documentation, by changing rules often, by approving for short windows, by demanding unnecessary steps, or by counting on the fact that most denials will not be appealed. The line between prudent review and friction as strategy is not always visible from the outside. Sometimes it may not even be visible to the people inside the organization. A metric that rewards lower utilization can sound responsible until the missing care appears in an emergency department months later.

The Provider Office as Authorization Department

Every PA requirement creates work somewhere. Usually, much of that work lands in the provider office. Medical assistants, nurses, billing staff, referral coordinators, pharmacists, and physicians chase forms, upload notes, answer questions, schedule P2P calls, track expiration dates, resubmit requests, and explain delays to patients.

This work is not incidental. It is a parallel administrative practice attached to the clinical practice. A primary care physician may spend the morning treating diabetes, hypertension, depression, back pain, and heart failure. Down the hall, staff are proving to half a dozen plans that the medications, scans, and referrals from last week were not whims. The chart is no longer only a record of care. It is evidence for a future argument.

Large health systems can build departments to handle this. Small practices often cannot. A rural clinic may have one person answering phones, scheduling referrals, rooming patients, and handling authorizations. A psychiatry practice may not have the staff to spend an hour on a medication denial. A physical therapy office may decide not to accept certain plans because the authorization process makes the business impossible. The burden falls unevenly, and that unevenness affects access.

There is also a morale cost. Clinicians did not enter medicine to become supplicants before portals. They understand accountability. They understand that not every requested service is appropriate. What wears them down is the sense that their trained judgment is being questioned by an invisible process that does not know the patient, that uses criteria they cannot easily see, and that can force them to choose between spending time with the patient in the room and fighting for the patient who left yesterday.

Patients feel the morale cost too. When the doctor says, "Your insurance denied it," the patient may hear that the plan does not care. When the plan says, "We need more information from your doctor," the patient may hear that the office dropped the ball. The truth may be that both sides are trying to work through a badly designed channel. But anger needs a target, and PA provides several.

The Patient as Messenger

In a well-designed system, the patient would not be the courier of administrative confusion. In our system, patients often become exactly that. The pharmacy tells them to call the doctor. The doctor tells them the request was sent. The plan tells them it is waiting for records. The vendor tells them the provider must use a different portal. The employer tells them to call the number on the card. The patient repeats the same story to every person and learns just enough vocabulary to remain trapped.

This messenger role is not harmless. It favors educated, persistent, English-speaking patients with flexible jobs, reliable phones, internet access, and family support. It punishes patients with limited health literacy, limited English proficiency, cognitive impairment, unstable housing, hourly work, transportation problems, or simple exhaustion. PA is often discussed as if it were a transaction between provider and payer. In practice, it can become a test of the patient's stamina.

A middle-class patient with a laptop and a flexible employer may fight through a denial. A patient working two jobs may not. A retired teacher may keep a notebook of call reference numbers. A patient with depression may give up after the first rejection. A parent with a medically complex child may become an expert in authorization because there is no other choice. The system calls this navigation. Sometimes it is just survival.

We should be blunt about what this means. Any authorization process that depends on patient persistence as a safety valve will worsen inequity. The patients least able to fight will lose most often. The denials that should be overturned will remain denials. The delays that should be escalated will remain delays. The care that should have happened will become one more bad outcome attributed to noncompliance.

There are few words in healthcare more dangerous than noncompliance. Sometimes it means the patient chose not to follow a reasonable plan. Sometimes it means the patient could not afford the medication, could not get the authorization, could not find transportation, could not understand the instructions, or could not spend three hours on the phone while also earning rent. PA can turn an administrative barrier into a clinical label.

Continuity of Care and the Annual Reset

Prior authorization is especially disruptive when patients change plans. A treatment that was approved in December may require a new authorization in January. A medication that kept a disease stable for years may be questioned because the new plan's formulary or policy is different. A new insurer may require step therapy even when the old insurer already watched the patient fail the required drug. The patient experiences this as absurd because it is absurd from the standpoint of the disease. The disease did not reset on January 1.

Plans will argue that they cannot be bound forever by another payer's decisions. That is true. A new plan has its own contract, network, formulary, and coverage policies. It needs the right to review high-cost or high-risk care. But continuity deserves special protection. If a patient is stable on a therapy, the burden should be high before disrupting it. A transition period should be real, not theoretical. Documentation from prior treatment should travel with the patient. The new plan should not force clinical backsliding in order to establish administrative authority.

This issue is especially important in mental health, autoimmune disease, cancer, epilepsy, transplant medicine, HIV treatment, and other areas where interruption can cause relapse, resistance, hospitalization, or loss of trust. A patient who has fought for months to become stable should not have to fight the same battle every enrollment cycle.

The same continuity problem appears when a drug is moved to a different formulary tier, when a provider leaves a network, when a plan delegates review to a new vendor, or when a policy is updated. The patient may not know that any of this happened. She simply discovers that the refill no longer goes through.

Gold Cards and Trust

One reform idea is often called gold carding. Under a gold-card approach, providers with high approval rates or strong adherence to evidence-based criteria are exempted from PA for certain services. The logic is simple: if a physician or facility almost always requests care that is ultimately approved, repeated front-end review may be wasteful. Trust should be earned and then operationalized.

Gold carding has appeal because it recognizes that not all providers behave the same way. Some have excellent documentation and conservative ordering patterns. Others order high-cost services at unusually high rates or submit requests that frequently fail criteria. Treating both groups identically may be administratively easy but clinically and economically foolish.

Still, gold carding is not magic. It can be gamed. It can create unfair advantages for large systems that have better data infrastructure. It can leave small practices behind. It can be granted too broadly and then quietly withdrawn. It can also become another opaque score that providers do not understand. If gold carding is used, the rules for earning it and losing it should be clear, specialty-sensitive, and publicly accountable.

The deeper principle is that PA should be targeted. A plan should not require authorization for a service simply because it can. It should require authorization because the service is costly, risky, frequently overused, highly variable, preference-sensitive, prone to fraud, or likely to be more appropriate in a different setting. Every PA list should have an expiration date. If a requirement does not meaningfully change behavior or improve value, it should be removed.

Electronic Prior Authorization and the Promise of Less Friction

A major part of current reform focuses on *electronic prior authorization* (ePA). The idea is not complicated: replace fax, phone, and manual portal work with standardized electronic transactions that can tell providers what is required, submit the necessary information, return decisions, and display denial reasons more efficiently.

The technical details are complicated. CMS's 2024 final rule requires certain impacted payers to implement application programming interfaces, or *application programming interface* (API) connections, including requirements built around Health

Level 7 Fast Healthcare Interoperability Resources, better known as *Fast Healthcare Interoperability Resources* (FHIR). These tools are meant to make information flow more easily among patients, providers, and payers. That is the right direction.

But electronic PA can fail if it merely digitizes a bad process. A faxed maze turned into an online maze is still a maze. A portal that asks the same unnecessary questions faster has not solved the real problem. A black-box API that returns a denial without usable explanation is not transparency. A requirement to upload fifty pages of notes electronically is not simplification if the reviewer needed only three facts.

CAQH has identified meaningful savings and time opportunities from administrative automation, including the electronic standard for prior authorization. Its 2024 Index key takeaways reported an opportunity to save the industry $515 million annually and save medical providers and staff 14 minutes per authorization by adopting the electronic standard.[114]

Those savings matter. Fourteen minutes multiplied across millions of requests is not a rounding error. But the more important measure is not only time saved by the submitter. It is whether the patient receives the right answer sooner. An electronic wrong answer is still wrong. An electronic delay is still a delay. Automation should be judged by accuracy, clarity, turnaround, appeal rates, patient outcomes, and administrative burden, not by speed alone.

Real-Time Benefit Tools and the Pharmacy Counter

A related technology is the *real-time benefit tool* (RTBT). In theory, an RTBT can tell a prescriber, while the patient is still in the office, whether a medication is covered, what the patient's cost may be, whether PA is required, and what alternatives may be preferred. That is exactly the kind of information that should exist before the patient reaches the pharmacy counter.

Imagine how different James's experience in Chapter 9 would feel if his physician could see during the visit that the prescribed drug required PA, that the plan preferred a different drug, that James had already failed the preferred drug, and that the necessary lab result was in the chart. The request could be submitted before James drove to the pharmacy. The pharmacist would not have to become the messenger. James would not learn about the problem through a rejected claim at the counter.

The promise is real, but so are the limitations. Cost estimates may be inaccurate. Formularies change. Patient accumulators and deductibles can be hard to calculate. The prescriber may not have time to compare every alternative during a crowded

---

[114] Council for Affordable Quality Healthcare, "2024 CAQH Index Key Takeaways: From Transactions to Trust," accessed online.

visit. The tool may favor the plan's preferred drug without showing why the preference exists. Manufacturer coupons and copay assistance may complicate the picture further.

Still, the direction is right. The system should not wait until the patient stands at a pharmacy counter to reveal that coverage is conditional. That is not a benefit design. That is a trapdoor.

The Ethics of Medical Necessity

The phrase medical necessity sounds objective, as if the service either is necessary or is not. Sometimes that is true. Antibiotics are not medically necessary for a viral cold. A wheelchair is medically necessary for a patient who cannot safely walk and meets coverage criteria. But many cases live in between.

Is a newer migraine drug medically necessary if older drugs helped a little but caused intolerable fatigue? Is a breast MRI medically necessary for a woman whose formal risk score is just below the cutoff but whose family history is frightening? Is inpatient rehabilitation medically necessary for a stroke patient who could technically go to a skilled nursing facility but would likely improve faster with intensive therapy? Is a biologic medically necessary when the patient has not failed every cheaper therapy, but the physician believes further delay will damage joints?

Medical necessity is not simply a scientific fact. It is a judgment made from evidence, patient circumstances, benefit language, policy choices, and resource limits. That does not mean it is arbitrary. It means the judgment should be explicit. A payer should be willing to say not only "this does not meet criteria," but why the criteria exist, what evidence would change the answer, and what alternative is being offered.

The ethical failure of PA is often not the existence of a no. It is the vagueness of the no. Patients and physicians can sometimes accept disagreement. What they cannot accept is a refusal that hides behind phrases like insufficient medical necessity without explaining what is insufficient. A denial should be a map to the missing bridge, not a wall with official letterhead.

There is a similar ethical obligation on the provider side. A physician who believes a service is necessary should document the reasons in a way that another clinician can understand. A request that says only "failed conservative therapy" is weaker than a request that explains what was tried, when, for how long, why it failed, and what risk the patient faces without escalation. The plan should not require an essay for every request, but when the case is complex, the record should tell the truth clearly.

Prior Authorization and Emergency Care

Emergency care operates under different rules. A patient with a stroke, heart attack, ruptured appendix, sepsis, or major trauma does not wait for a portal determination. Federal emergency treatment obligations and basic decency require evaluation and stabilization. Yet authorization issues do not disappear from emergency and urgent care. They reappear around admissions, transfers, observation status, post-acute placement, imaging follow-up, and medications after discharge.

An emergency physician may decide that a patient needs admission. The hospital may notify the plan. The plan may later question whether inpatient status was necessary or whether observation would have been appropriate. That is not technically the same as requiring pre-approval before emergency care, but it affects hospital behavior. If plans repeatedly deny inpatient admissions after the fact, hospitals respond by building utilization review teams that scrutinize status while the patient is still in the bed.

This is another example of the maze moving upstream. A retrospective denial becomes concurrent review. Concurrent review becomes pressure at the bedside. The patient thinks she is being admitted because she is sick. The hospital is also asking whether the record will support the level of care when the payer reviews it.

For post-acute care, PA can delay discharge. A patient recovering from a hip fracture may be ready to leave the hospital but unsafe to go home. The rehabilitation facility needs authorization. The plan needs records. The hospital sends therapy notes. The family waits. If the denial comes, the discharge plan changes. If the approval comes late, the bed may be gone. The hospital stay lengthens, not because the patient needs more hospital medicine, but because the next door has not opened.

The Administrative Burden as Clinical Risk

The burden of PA is often described in dollars and hours. That is appropriate, but incomplete. Administrative burden can become clinical risk. A patient who waits for imaging may have a delayed diagnosis. A patient who cannot obtain medication may deteriorate. A patient whose surgery is postponed may live with pain longer and use more opioids. A patient whose mental health medication is interrupted may relapse. A patient whose rehabilitation stay is denied may fall at home.

Not every bad outcome after a PA delay was caused by PA. Medicine is complicated, and diseases progress despite everyone's best efforts. But the system should not hide behind that complexity. If a process predictably delays care for large numbers of people, some of those delays will matter clinically. A health plan cannot claim credit for avoided waste while treating delayed harm as anecdote.

Measurement is difficult. How do you count the patient who never filled the prescription? How do you count the cancer patient whose treatment started ten days late? How do you count the worker who lost wages during the delay? How do you count the child whose parent spent hours on authorization calls instead of at work or asleep? Some harms leave claims. Some leave only fatigue.

The system tends to count what is easy: requests submitted, requests approved, requests denied, turnaround time, appeals, reversals. It struggles to count what matters more: anxiety, abandonment, clinical deterioration, lost trust, and the quiet decision not to seek care next time because the last attempt was too exhausting.

Prior Authorization and Medical Bills

At first glance, PA may seem separate from the medical bill. It happens before care. Bills arrive after care. In reality, PA and billing are tightly connected. An authorization number can determine whether a claim is paid. A service performed without required authorization may be denied even if the care was medically reasonable. A site-of-care authorization may determine whether the patient pays outpatient hospital coinsurance or a lower office-based amount. A drug authorization may determine whether a product is covered under the pharmacy benefit, the medical benefit, or not at all.

This connection is one of the most confusing parts for patients. Many people think approval means the service will be paid in full. It usually does not. Authorization is not a guarantee of payment. The claim still has to be submitted. Eligibility still has to be valid on the date of service. The provider still has to be in network if network status matters. The code still has to match. Deductibles and coinsurance still apply. Other plan limitations may still exist.

That sentence - authorization is not a guarantee of payment - may be legally necessary. It is also maddening. The patient hears yes and assumes yes means yes. The system hears yes and means, "This service appears to meet certain coverage rules, subject to eligibility, benefits, coding, contract terms, claim submission requirements, and other limitations." One of those statements belongs to ordinary human language. The other belongs to the labyrinth.

A better system would tell the patient what the authorization means and does not mean in plain language. It would say: this request has been approved for this service, by this provider, at this location, during this date range; based on current information, your estimated responsibility is this amount; the estimate may change if your eligibility changes, if the service changes, if additional services are performed, or if the claim is coded differently. That is not perfect, but it is far better than a mysterious authorization number.

A Tale of Two Denials

Let us imagine two denials.

In the first, a healthy 42-year-old man asks for a full-body screening MRI because he saw an advertisement. He has no symptoms, no relevant family history, and no clinical finding that suggests disease. The plan denies the request. The denial says the requested scan is not covered because there is no evidence of medical necessity and because full-body screening MRI in asymptomatic adults can lead to false positives, unnecessary follow-up, and potential harm. It tells the patient that routine preventive care remains covered and tells the physician what clinical findings would support targeted imaging.

That denial may frustrate the patient. It is also defensible.

In the second, a 42-year-old woman with a prior cancer history develops persistent back pain, night pain, and a new neurologic symptom. Her physician orders an MRI and sends an office note that mentions back pain but fails to include the cancer history and neurologic change. The plan denies the request because conservative therapy has not been documented. The patient waits three weeks before the missing information is recognized and the denial is overturned.

That denial may also be technically explainable. It is not defensible in the same way. The record was incomplete, yes. But the process did not protect the patient from the consequence of incompleteness. It converted a documentation gap into delayed diagnosis risk.

The difference between those cases is the difference between PA as stewardship and PA as machinery. Stewardship asks the right question and gives a clear answer. Machinery processes what it receives and calls the result a decision.

What Better Prior Authorization Would Look Like

A better PA system would begin with discipline about what requires authorization. Plans should be required, or at least expected, to justify PA lists with evidence of cost, variation, safety concern, overuse, fraud risk, or site-of-care opportunity. Requirements should be reviewed regularly and retired when they no longer add value. A service that is approved 98 percent of the time should not remain on a PA list unless the remaining 2 percent represent serious risk.

Second, the requirements should be discoverable before the order is placed. The physician should not need to guess. The electronic health record should be able to ask the plan, in real time, whether the service requires PA, what documentation is required, what alternatives are preferred, and what patient cost implications may exist. This information should be available in the normal clinical workflow, not buried in a PDF policy last updated six months ago.

Third, the request should ask only for information needed to decide. If the policy turns on three facts, the system should ask for those three facts. It should not demand the entire chart. It should not force staff to upload documents that no one will read. It should not ask for information the payer already has, such as recent claims showing prior medication failure, unless there is a legitimate reason the claims are insufficient.

Fourth, approval should be durable enough to be useful. An authorization that expires before the patient can schedule the service creates needless rework. A chronic medication approval should not require constant reauthorization when the diagnosis is permanent and the patient is stable. A treatment plan involving multiple cycles or visits should be authorized in a way that matches clinical reality.

Fifth, denials should be specific. "Not medically necessary" is not enough. The denial should identify the criterion not met, the evidence reviewed, the information missing, the alternative if any, the appeal rights, and the fastest path to correction. If a medical director made the decision, that should be clear. If a vendor made the decision under delegated authority, that should be clear too.

Sixth, urgent requests should be truly urgent. The system should not define urgency so narrowly that only a patient already in crisis qualifies. At the same time, providers should not label every request urgent merely to jump the line. Abuse of urgency slows the cases that genuinely need speed. Integrity is required on both sides.

Seventh, continuity should be protected. Stable patients should not be forced into avoidable interruptions because the calendar changed, the plan changed, or a vendor contract changed. If a plan wants to revisit therapy, it should provide a transition period and a clinically reasonable process.

Eighth, appeals should be simple enough that patients can actually use them. A right that cannot be exercised is mostly decoration. Appeal instructions should be readable. Deadlines should be clear. Assistance should be available. Urgent appeals should move quickly. External review should be meaningful, not merely another waiting room.

Ninth, performance should be public. Plans should report PA volume, approval rates, denial rates, turnaround times, appeal rates, reversal rates, and categories of service in ways that employers, regulators, providers, and patients can understand. Data alone will not fix the problem, but hidden performance will preserve it.

Tenth, the patient should not be the system's messenger. The provider, payer, pharmacy, and vendor should communicate directly through shared standards. The patient should be informed, not conscripted.

Where Artificial Intelligence Fits

Artificial intelligence will inevitably enter PA. In some places, it already has. The same tools that can summarize records, extract lab values, match criteria, and draft letters can also be used to approve, deny, or route authorization requests. This is both promising and dangerous.

The promise is obvious. AI could read the policy and the record, identify the facts that matter, alert the provider to missing information before submission, recommend approval when criteria are clearly met, and produce a plain-language explanation for the patient. It could reduce the need for repeated faxing, manual note review, and P2P calls over missing facts. It could make the first answer better.

The danger is equally obvious. AI could become a faster denial machine. It could learn from flawed historical decisions. It could apply criteria without nuance. It could hide reasoning behind technical language. It could shift accountability away from humans. It could make patients and physicians feel that they are arguing with a wall that has learned to speak.

The rule should be straightforward: AI may assist prior authorization, but it should not become unaccountable prior authorization. Decisions must be explainable, appealable, auditable, and supervised by qualified humans. The patient and provider should be able to know why the answer was reached and what evidence would change it. A machine can help find the thread. It should not become the Minotaur.

If used well, AI could support the independent translation layer discussed in the final chapter. The same evidence map that supports claim payment could support PA. Before the service is rendered, the system could ask: is the patient eligible, is the benefit available, is authorization required, what criteria apply, what does the record show, what is missing, what is the expected patient cost, and what explanation should be provided?

That would not eliminate hard choices. Some services would still be denied. Some policies would still be disputed. Some patients would still disagree with the answer. But disagreement with an understandable answer is better than confusion before an invisible one.

The Human Test

The final test of PA should not be whether it saves money. Saving money is important, but money is not the only value in healthcare. The test should be whether PA saves money in ways that are clinically sound, administratively efficient, transparent, and fair to the people who are sick.

A PA program that prevents unnecessary full-body scans, unsafe drug combinations, duplicative procedures, or overpriced sites of care may be doing real good. A PA program that repeatedly delays cancer drugs, interrupts stable chronic therapy, denies rehabilitation without meaningful review, or forces patients to abandon treatment because the process is exhausting is not stewardship. It is rationing by hassle.

Every health system rations. Some ration by price. Some ration by queue. Some ration by geography. Some ration by public policy. The United States often rations by complexity. That is the least honest method because it allows everyone to deny that rationing is happening. The care was not refused, exactly. It was pending. It was missing information. It was out of network. It required another step. It was not appealed in time. It was abandoned.

A humane PA process would be honest about scarcity, careful about evidence, respectful of clinicians, understandable to patients, and humble about its own errors. It would recognize that every pending request belongs to a person whose life is not pending.

Denise eventually receives her answer. In one possible version of the story, the drug is approved that afternoon, the infusion is rescheduled, and the delay is only an awful day. In another, the request is denied, the oncologist appeals, the plan reverses itself, and the treatment starts two weeks later. In another, the denial stands, and the doctor chooses a different regimen. In another, Denise gives up on understanding the process and follows whatever path is placed in front of her because fighting the system takes strength she needs for the disease.

The health plan does not see all of those versions. It sees a request, a decision, a turnaround time, a denial reason, an appeal status, and a claim if care occurs. The provider sees a patient, a record, a staff burden, a treatment plan, and a fight. Denise sees the refrigerator where the medicine might be, the chair where she might sit, and the calendar where another day has been crossed out.

Prior authorization sits before the claim, before the bill, before the EOB, before the appeal of a denied claim. It is the wall around medical care that must be climbed before the care can happen. If the wall must exist, there should be gates that open quickly when the path is clear, explain itself when it stays closed, and never forget that a person is waiting on the other side.

Small Doors, Big Consequences

The examples we have used so far involve large and obvious moments: cancer treatment, surgery, MRI scans, rehabilitation, and specialty drugs. Those are the cases that make PA visible. They produce urgent phone calls and angry emails because the stakes are unmistakable. Yet some of the most corrosive effects of PA come from smaller interruptions repeated over time. A child cannot get a rescue inhaler because the plan prefers a different formulation. A diabetic patient cannot obtain the continuous glucose monitor supplies on time because a supplier needs a new authorization. A patient with sleep apnea waits for a replacement mask while daytime exhaustion returns. A person recovering from a stroke loses therapy visits because the next set has not been approved. None of these examples may look catastrophic on a spreadsheet. All of them can change a life for a while.

Small delays also accumulate in bodies. A week without the right inhaler can mean an emergency visit. A month without therapy can mean loss of function that is hard to regain. A missed infusion can mean a flare. A delayed wheelchair repair can mean a person stays in bed, then becomes weaker, then needs more care. The medical record may later describe the decline as progression of disease or deconditioning. That description may be accurate, but it may omit the administrative push that started the slide.

This is one of the reasons patients become so angry. They are not merely upset that a form was required. They are upset because the form seems to have more power than the symptom. The plan may be asking for information to ensure appropriate use. The patient experiences it as a stranger interrupting the treatment plan that was worked out with a clinician who knows them. Both understandings can be true, but the patient is the one who bears the consequences while the understanding is sorted out.

For people with chronic illness, PA can also disrupt the fragile routines that make disease manageable. A patient who finally found a migraine regimen that allows him to work may live in fear of the renewal date. A mother whose child has severe eczema may keep a folder of photographs, failed creams, visit notes, and previous approvals. A man with heart failure may know the names of his medications and still not understand why the new dose requires a new request. Healthcare often asks patients to be disciplined, adherent, and responsible. Then the payment system interrupts the very routines it tells them to maintain.

The effect on mental health deserves special attention. A patient with depression, anxiety, bipolar disorder, schizophrenia, or substance use disorder may already struggle with the tasks of daily life. Requiring that person to chase an authorization, navigate a denial, or tolerate a forced medication switch can be more than inconvenient. It can destabilize care. In behavioral health, trust and continuity are not luxuries. They are part of the treatment. A process that repeatedly interrupts medications or therapy visits can undo progress that took months to build.

Prior authorization can be especially cruel when the patient cannot see the reason for the rule. A patient may understand why an insurer asks questions before approving an experimental treatment. It is harder to understand why a long-standing medication suddenly requires proof again. It is harder still to understand why the proof must be supplied by a doctor who has already supplied it before, to a plan that already paid for the same medication last month. A system that requires repetition should be able to explain why repetition is necessary. Often, it cannot.

The Employer in the Background

Most discussions of PA frame the conflict as provider versus payer, with the patient caught between them. That frame misses another actor: the employer. For many Americans, the health plan is part of compensation. The employer may be paying premiums to an insurance company, or it may be self-funded and paying claims directly while hiring an administrator to run the plan. Either way, the employer has a financial interest in controlling healthcare costs.

An employer does not usually want employees to be denied needed care. A company wants workers healthy, present, productive, and loyal. It does not help a business when an employee misses work because a medication was delayed or a surgery was canceled at the last minute. At the same time, the employer sees the annual health benefit renewal and knows that uncontrolled spending can raise premiums, reduce wages, shrink hiring, or force cuts in other benefits. In this sense, PA is one of the hidden ways employers try to buy affordability.

This creates a difficult moral triangle. The employee wants care. The employer wants a sustainable benefit. The plan or administrator wants to manage spending and fulfill its contract. The doctor wants to treat the patient. Each participant can defend its position. None of them may feel responsible for the whole experience. The patient experiences all of them as one system because the patient does not have the luxury of separating benefit design, claims administration, vendor delegation, and medical necessity review.

Employers should therefore ask better questions about PA than simply whether it saves money. They should ask how many requests are required, how many are approved, how long decisions take, how often denials are appealed, how often appeals are reversed, which services are most affected, and what employees experience when they try to use the benefit. They should ask whether PA is being used for high-value targets or spread across too many routine services. They should ask whether the plan protects continuity of care. They should ask whether a denial reason can be understood by an ordinary person.

This is not sentimental advice. It is hard-nosed management. A benefit that looks efficient on a spreadsheet may be expensive in absenteeism, turnover, lost productivity, and employee resentment. A parent who spends six hours trying to obtain authorization for a child's medication is not bringing her full attention to work. A worker who abandons treatment because the process is exhausting may later have a more expensive medical crisis. A health plan can save a dollar in one column and create three dollars of cost in another.

The same point applies to public programs. A Medicaid program or Medicare Advantage plan that uses PA to manage spending must also consider the downstream costs of delay, confusion, and abandonment. Government budgets, like employer budgets, can be tempted by visible savings and blind to dispersed harms. The patient, of course, does not experience the costs as dispersed. They all arrive in one life.

The Documentation Burden Returns

PA also loops back to one of the book's recurring themes: documentation. In the claim world, documentation supports codes. In the PA world, documentation supports permission. The physician note must contain the facts the payer policy wants to see. If the note is clinically clear to the treating physician but lacks the policy's required terms, the request may fail. The patient may have severe pain, but the policy asks whether the pain limits activities of daily living. The patient may have tried medication, but the policy asks for the medication name, dose, duration, and reason for discontinuation. The doctor may know the answer. The record may not prove it.

This creates another incentive. Doctors and staff learn to document for authorization. They add phrases that match policies. They list failed therapies in structured ways. They create templates. Sometimes this improves clarity. Sometimes it turns the medical record into a pleading document. The note is no longer written only for the next clinician. It is written for the payer reviewer who may read it under time pressure and search for required words.

Again, the behavior is rational. If a plan requires documentation of six weeks of conservative therapy, the office will learn to write exactly that. If a plan requires the phrase moderate to severe, the phrase will appear. If a plan requires a score from a depression scale or a psoriasis area measure, that number will be documented. The danger is that the record can begin to reflect what the policy rewards more than what the patient needs. The same distortion we saw with coding can appear before the claim.

A good PA system would not punish clear clinical narrative simply because it does not match a rigid template. It would also not require reviewers to infer key facts from vague notes. The best path is structured clarity: ask for the information that matters, make it easy to provide, and let the clinician add nuance when the case does not fit the template. The system should support honest documentation, not incantation.

Patients can help by knowing their own histories, but the burden should not be theirs alone. A patient may remember that a medication failed but not the dose. She may remember physical therapy but not the exact dates. She may remember that an MRI was done at another facility but not have the report. Plans and providers already possess enormous amounts of data. A more humane system would use that data responsibly rather than forcing patients to reconstruct their medical lives from memory.

When No One Is Lying

Some of the hardest PA disputes occur when no one is lying. The provider genuinely believes the service is needed. The payer genuinely believes the policy is not met. The patient genuinely believes the delay is harmful. The reviewer genuinely believes the record is incomplete. Everyone may be acting in good faith, and the result may still be miserable.

This matters because healthcare debates too often collapse into villain stories. The insurer is greedy. The doctor is gaming the system. The patient is demanding unnecessary care. The vendor is hiding behind algorithms. Sometimes those stories are true enough to matter. There are bad actors. There are financial incentives that warp behavior. There are denials that should not happen and requests that should never have been made. But much of the daily misery of PA comes from ordinary people following rules that were not designed around the full human journey.

A nurse reviewer may see an incomplete request and follow policy by asking for more information. The office staff may have sent what they had and may not know why the plan says it is incomplete. The physician may be seeing twenty patients and may not be reachable for a P2P until the end of the day. The patient may have already taken off work for the test. The plan may still meet its turnaround requirement. Every step may be defensible. The whole experience may be indefensible.

This is why process design is moral work. A badly designed process can make decent people behave in ways that injure trust. It can make a nurse sound uncaring, a doctor sound evasive, a patient sound demanding, and a plan sound cruel. The fix is not merely to ask everyone to be nicer on the phone. The fix is to reduce the number of unnecessary phone calls, make the rules visible, route the right information the first time, and give each person enough authority to solve the problem in front of them.

The False Comfort of Approval Rates

Plans sometimes defend PA by noting that most requests are approved. That may be true. It may also miss the point. A high approval rate can mean that PA is working because providers submit appropriate requests and inappropriate requests are filtered out. It can also mean that PA is being required for too many services that almost always meet criteria, creating work without value. If 98 of 100 requests are approved, the important question is what was learned from making all 100 pass through the gate.

Denial rates can be misleading in the other direction. A low denial rate may hide care that was never requested because the provider knew the rule would be too difficult. It may hide patients who abandoned care at the pharmacy counter before an authorization was submitted. It may hide substitutions made to avoid the process. It may hide the physician who chose a less effective alternative because fighting for the preferred one would take too long. The absence of a denial is not the same as the presence of access.

Appeal rates are also hard to interpret. A low appeal rate might mean the initial denials were correct. It might mean patients and providers lack the time, knowledge, or energy to appeal. A high reversal rate might mean the appeal process works. It might mean the initial process fails. Numbers need context. They need to be connected to patient outcomes, provider burden, and the reasons behind decisions.

This is why public reporting must be thoughtful. Raw approval and denial rates are useful, but not enough. Reports should distinguish service categories, urgent versus standard requests, initial requests versus renewals, new therapy versus continuation therapy, provider type, line of business, and outcome after appeal. Otherwise, PA metrics become another set of numbers that can be technically true and practically misleading.

A Practical Covenant

What should patients be able to expect? They should expect to know when PA is required. They should expect that their doctor and plan can communicate without using them as the messenger. They should expect a timely decision. They should expect a clear reason if the answer is no. They should expect that urgent situations are handled urgently. They should expect that stable treatment is not casually interrupted. They should expect that the appeal path is real. They should expect that the people designing the process remember that illness is already work.

What should providers be able to expect? They should expect rules that are available, current, clinically sensible, and specific. They should expect electronic submission that works. They should expect that a complete request receives an answer without repeated calls. They should expect that P2P review involves a qualified clinician with authority to act. They should expect that their strong performance can reduce unnecessary review. They should also expect to document clearly and to accept that not every requested service will be covered.

What should payers be able to expect? They should expect providers to submit honest, complete information. They should expect that high-cost, risky, or highly variable care can be reviewed. They should expect employers, regulators, and patients to recognize that benefit dollars are finite. They should also expect to be held accountable for delays, vague denials, excessive requirements, and review processes that create more harm than value.

That mutual set of expectations is not a contract in the legal sense. It is a practical covenant. It says that prior authorization, if it exists, must serve care rather than merely control it. It says that stewardship is honorable only when it remains connected to the person waiting. It says that financial responsibility and clinical responsibility should not be enemies.

The American healthcare system often fails because each participant optimizes its own small part of the maze. The provider optimizes documentation. The payer optimizes utilization. The employer optimizes benefit cost. The vendor optimizes workflow volume. The patient optimizes survival. A better PA system would force those optimizations to meet at a shared point: the right care, at the right time, with a truthful explanation of who pays and why.

That standard will not eliminate conflict. It will make conflict more honest. And in the labyrinth, honest conflict is progress.

A Word About Responsibility

Responsibility in PA is scattered. The patient is responsible for following up. The physician is responsible for documenting. The office staff is responsible for submitting. The payer is responsible for deciding. The vendor is responsible for processing. The employer or public program is responsible for the benefit design. The regulator is responsible for setting minimum protections. Each responsibility can be defended on its own. Yet when the process fails, the scattering becomes a hiding place. Everyone can point to the next person in the chain.

A better system would not remove responsibility. It would concentrate accountability at the points where decisions are actually made. If the plan requires authorization, the plan should be accountable for making the requirement easy to identify and the decision easy to understand. If the provider orders the service, the provider should be accountable for sending a record that explains the need. If a vendor acts for the plan, the plan should remain accountable for the vendor. If a patient is asked to participate in an appeal, the instructions should be clear enough that participation is realistic.

This is especially important when a denial is based on missing information. Missing information is not always the provider's fault. It may be missing because the payer asked the wrong question, because the portal did not accept the file, because the requested data live in another system, because the patient changed doctors, or because the policy asks for a detail that was not clinically important at the time of the visit. A good reviewer should distinguish between a record that does not support the request and a process that failed to gather the right evidence.

The patient should not pay the price for that distinction being ignored. If the missing information is easily obtainable, the process should seek it before denying. If the missing information is irrelevant to the outcome, it should not be required. If the missing information is truly essential, the denial should say exactly what is missing and how to provide it. The goal should be a correct answer, not a defensible stop sign.

The Language Problem

PA also suffers from a language problem. Plans use words like medical necessity, benefit exclusion, insufficient documentation, experimental, not clinically appropriate, non-covered service, and out of network. Providers use words like failed therapy, refractory disease, worsening symptoms, high risk, urgent, and standard of care. Patients use words like pain, fear, work, sleep, walking, breathing, and getting through the day. These are not separate languages because people are being difficult. They are separate languages because each participant is standing in a different part of the maze.

The best authorization systems translate among these languages. They do not force the patient to learn insurance language just to understand why a treatment is delayed. They do not force the doctor to guess which policy phrase will unlock the answer. They do not force the payer reviewer to dig through twenty pages to find the two facts that matter. They put the clinical question, the coverage rule, and the patient consequence in the same frame.

For example, instead of a denial that says the request does not meet medical necessity criteria, a useful denial might say: the plan covers this medication for this diagnosis after two preferred medications have been tried for at least eight weeks each or are medically inappropriate; the records show one preferred medication was tried; the records do not show a second trial or a reason a second preferred medication cannot be used; please submit documentation of the second trial, contraindication, adverse reaction, or other clinical reason. That is still a denial. It is also a path.

The same approach could help approvals. An approval should not be a cryptic authorization number with hidden boundaries. It should say what was approved, for whom, by whom, where, for how long, and under what limits. It should tell the patient whether the approval affects cost-sharing or merely coverage. It should tell the provider whether the authorization covers related services or only the primary code. Plain language does not weaken the system. It strengthens trust.

Why Prior Authorization Matters

Prior authorization gathers almost every theme we have explored. It depends on codes, because the requested service must be identified. It depends on benefits, because the plan must decide whether the service is covered. It depends on contracts, because network status and site of care matter. It depends on documentation, because the record must support the request. It depends on technology, because portals and electronic transactions shape the experience. It depends on ethics, because delay and denial affect real people. It depends on economics, because unlimited payment is not possible.

In other words, PA is not a side alley. It is one of the main corridors of the modern labyrinth. The patient may enter it before receiving care, then enter the billing maze afterward. A service may be authorized and still billed confusingly. A service may be denied before it happens and never produce a claim at all. A medication may be switched to avoid PA, changing both clinical care and future cost. The absence of a bill does not mean the absence of harm. Sometimes the missing bill represents care that never occurred.

That is why reforming medical bills without reforming prior authorization would leave an important door locked. A clear bill after delayed care is not enough. A fair payment after an unnecessary fight is not enough. Honest translation has to begin before the claim exists. It has to start when the doctor says, this is what I recommend, and the patient asks, can we do it?

The wall around care must therefore be judged by the same standard as the bill after care: does it clarify the truth, or does it hide it?

Chapter 10: Breadcrumbs for the Labyrinth

- Prior authorization is a pre-service coverage decision that asks whether a requested service, drug, device, setting, or level of care should be covered before the claim exists.
- PA can be a legitimate utilization management tool when it prevents unsafe, duplicative, low-value, or unnecessarily costly care but becomes harmful when it is opaque, slow, overly broad, or poorly targeted.
- The health plan process usually includes eligibility checks, benefit review, code and diagnosis matching, documentation intake, clinician review, and communication of approval or denial.
- Peer-to-peer review can resolve real clinical nuance, but it becomes wasteful when it merely compensates for vague denials or incomplete first-pass review.
- Electronic PA, APIs, FHIR-based data exchange, real-time benefit tools, gold carding, clearer denial reasons, public metrics, and continuity protections can improve the process.
- The ethical test is whether prior authorization protects patients and shared resources without becoming rationing by delay, exhaustion, or confusion.

CHAPTER 11
FINDING THE THREAD IN THE LABYRINTH

It is a Tuesday morning, and Emily is sitting at her kitchen table with a cup of coffee, a laptop, two envelopes, and three browser tabs open.

She is not sick. That is what makes the morning so aggravating. The sickness was last month, when she had a spell of chest tightness, went to an urgent care center, was sent to a hospital emergency department, had blood tests, an electrocardiogram, a chest X-ray, and a few hours of observation, and then went home with the reassuring news that she had not had a heart attack.

Now the illness is gone, but the bills remain.

One envelope says, THIS IS NOT A BILL. Another looks very much like a bill but tells her that the amount due may change after insurance processes the claim. The hospital portal shows a balance that does not match either piece of paper. Her insurance portal says a claim was denied, then adjusted, then partially paid. One line mentions a facility charge. Another mentions a professional service. Another has a code she does not understand. A fourth line says the service was bundled into another service, which sounds as if it should be good news until she notices that the balance did not go away.

Emily is a capable person. She handles a household budget. She reads contracts before she signs them. She knows enough not to pay an unfamiliar invoice before checking it. Still, after thirty minutes, she has no idea what she owes, whom she owes, or why.

Somewhere away from Emily's kitchen table, the same encounter is being translated by other people and other machines. A coder has looked at the medical record. A billing system has produced claim lines. A clearinghouse has moved the data. A payer system has applied edits. A contract has converted allowed amounts into payments. A patient accounting system has pushed some remainder to Emily. If a line is denied, someone may appeal. If a code seems unsupported, someone may review the chart. If a balance is old enough, someone may send another letter.

Emily had one scare. The system produced an avalanche of forms, reports, and bills.

Making Things Better

That is where this book has been heading. The problem with modern medical bills is not merely that they are hard for patients to understand, though that is bad enough. The deeper problem is that the bill is now the visible end of an enormous translation machine. The machine takes the messy facts of illness and turns them into codes, edits, policies, contracts, payments, denials, appeals, balances, audits, and sometimes lawsuits. We built the machine because we needed consistency. We added to it because each prior solution left a new problem. We now live inside it because almost every participant depends on it.

The central question is no longer whether the system is complicated. That question has been answered.

The question is whether the complication is still buying us enough truth to justify its cost.

A long time ago, Thomas de Burgh's physician accepted payment in a world where the patient's status, the practitioner's education, and private custom mattered more than any public fee schedule. The arrangement was personal and opaque. It had the virtue of simplicity for the people who could afford it and the vice of arbitrariness for everyone else. Centuries later, my parents could pay a handwritten hospital bill for the birth of a child. That bill looks almost innocent now, not because the past was fairer, but because the old transaction could fit on one slip of paper.

The modern claim could not.

We have watched classification systems grow from Bertillon's list of causes of death into the ICD. We have watched Blue Cross and Blue Shield help separate hospital payment from physician payment. We have watched employer-based insurance become the dominant way Americans financed medical care. We have watched Medicare and Medicaid bring public financing to older Americans, people with disabilities, and the poor. We have watched cost-based reimbursement give way to prospective payment. We have watched DRGs, APR-DRGs, MS-DRGs, CCs, MCCs, SOIs, and ROMs convert clinical severity into payment levels. We have watched CPT and HCPCS standardize physician services, supplies, drugs, devices, and countless other services. We have watched OPPS, APCs, EAPGs, revenue codes, modifiers, NCCI edits, MUEs, claim forms, billing portals, payer policies, clearinghouses, contracts, prior authorization programs, step therapy rules, pharmacy benefit controls, and appeal processes pile onto the structure.

None of these layers was unwise at the moment of its birth. ICD allowed diseases to be counted and compared. CPT allowed services to be described consistently. DRGs put hospitals at financial risk for efficiency. Revenue codes organized facility charges. Edits prevented many duplicate or improper payments. CDI tried to make clinical documentation match the patient's true condition. PI tried to make payment match the record and the rules. RCM tried to help providers survive a payment environment so complex that merely getting paid became a specialized profession. Prior authorization tried to answer a different question before the claim ever existed:

should this requested service, drug, device, site of care, or level of care be covered for this patient under this plan at this moment?

The tragedy is that each good idea created new incentives. If a diagnosis changes payment, then documentation becomes financially important. If a modifier bypasses an edit, then the modifier becomes valuable. If one claim form asks for one kind of data and another asks for another kind, then the split itself becomes part of the strategy. If a payer denies based on opaque policy, a provider learns to bill around the opacity. If a provider bills around the opacity, the payer adds another edit. If the edit is too blunt, honest claims are denied. If it is too narrow, abusive claims slip through. The maze grows because everyone is responding rationally to the walls in front of them. If authorization becomes the door to treatment, then the doorway itself becomes a source of leverage, delay, anxiety, and sometimes harm.

It is tempting to blame the other side. Providers complain that payers deny first and explain later. Payers complain that providers code aggressively and appeal endlessly. Patients suspect that both sides speak in a language designed to keep ordinary people confused. Regulators add rules because someone, somewhere, found a way to exploit the last set of rules. Vendors promise relief, then become another layer that has to be paid for and governed.

There is truth in all of these complaints, but blame is not a plan.

The first honest step is to admit the size of the burden. In 2024, national health expenditures in the United States reached about $5.3 trillion, or $15,474 per person, and represented 18.0 percent of gross domestic product.[115] Even a small percentage of waste in a system that large is not small. Administrative expense is not a rounding error. Chernew and Mintz noted that administrative expenses are commonly estimated at 15 to 25 percent of total national health expenditures, amounting to hundreds of billions of dollars annually.[116] The Commonwealth Fund has similarly described administrative complexity as a major contributor to excess American health spending, with the United States spending far more per person on governance and financing administration than comparable high-income countries.[117]

This is the cost of getting to an answer.

---

[115] Centers for Medicare & Medicaid Services, "NHE Fact Sheet," CMS, accessed April 26, 2026, https://www.cms.gov/data-research/statistics-trends-and-reports/national-health-expenditure-data/nhe-fact-sheet.

[116] Michael E. Chernew and Harrison Mintz, "Administrative Expenses in the US Health Care System: Why So High?" JAMA 326, no. 17 (2021): 1679-1680, https://doi.org/10.1001/jama.2021.17318.

[117] David Blumenthal, Evan D. Gumas, and Arnav Shah, "Mirror, Mirror 2024: A Portrait of the Failing U.S. Health System," Commonwealth Fund, September 19, 2024, accessed April 26, 2026, https://www.commonwealthfund.org/publications/fund-reports/2024/sep/mirror-mirror-2024.

Some of that cost is necessary. A country that pays billions of claims cannot adjudicate each one in a town meeting. It needs codes, rules, standard formats, appeal rights, medical necessity policies, fraud controls, and people trained to apply all of them. We should not romanticize a world without administrative structure. A world without structure is a world where the powerful set prices in private and the weak hope for kindness.

But a necessary function can still become bloated. In 2021, McKinsey estimated that a set of known administrative simplification interventions could save the United States as much as $265 billion per year.[118] The *Council for Affordable Quality Healthcare* (CAQH), which studies routine healthcare transactions such as eligibility checks, claims status inquiries, prior authorizations, and payments, reported continuing multibillion-dollar opportunities from moving manual processes to electronic ones.[119] CMS itself, in a 2024 final rule on interoperability and prior authorization, estimated that its requirements would save roughly $15 billion over ten years by improving electronic prior authorization processes and requiring clearer denial explanations.[120] These numbers differ in scope and method, but they all point in the same direction: the payment machine consumes resources that could otherwise go toward care.

Denials are a useful example. Some denials are entirely appropriate. A claim may be a duplicate. A diagnosis may not support the service. A modifier may be wrong. A code may be unbundled in a way that violates the rules. Paying every submitted claim without review would be an invitation to error and fraud. At the same time, denial has become its own industry. In 2024, KFF reported that insurers in HealthCare.gov marketplace plans denied about one in five claims overall, with rates varying widely by insurer and claim type; the overwhelming majority of denied claims were not appealed.[121] That means many patients and providers simply absorb the answer, even when the answer may be wrong.

---

[118] Nikhil R. Sahni, Prakriti Mishra, Brandon Carrus, and David M. Cutler, "Administrative Simplification: How to Save a Quarter-Trillion Dollars in US Healthcare," McKinsey & Company, October 20, 2021, accessed April 26, 2026, https://www.mckinsey.com/industries/healthcare/our-insights/administrative-simplification-how-to-save-a-quarter-trillion-dollars-in-us-healthcare.

[119] CAQH, "2024 CAQH Index: Health Plans and Providers Can Save $20 Billion by Automating Administrative Transactions," February 11, 2025, accessed April 26, 2026, https://www.caqh.org/about/newsletter/2024-caqh-index-health-plans-and-providers-can-save-20-billion-automating-administrative-transactions.

[120] Centers for Medicare & Medicaid Services, "CMS Interoperability and Prior Authorization Final Rule (CMS-0057-F)," January 17, 2024, accessed April 26, 2026, https://www.cms.gov/priorities/burden-reduction/policies-and-regulations/cms-interoperability-and-prior-authorization-final-rule-cms-0057-f.

[121] Cynthia Cox, Krutika Amin, and Kaye Pestaina, "Claims Denials and Appeals in ACA Marketplace Plans in 2024," KFF, October 15, 2025, accessed April 26, 2026,

The same dynamic exists on the provider side. A hospital that cannot get claims paid on time cannot keep nurses, maintain operating rooms, buy medications, or keep the lights on. It builds a revenue cycle department. It hires coders. It trains CDI staff. It buys software. It contracts with RCM vendors. It appeals denials. It studies payer behavior. It does not do this because the people in charge love paperwork. It does it because payment is survival.

The payer responds in kind. It builds claims editing logic. It hires nurses, coders, physicians, actuaries, lawyers, and data scientists. It contracts with PI vendors. It develops prepayment and postpayment review programs. It audits provider behavior. It does not do this only because it wants to say no. It does it because claims data determine payment, and inaccurate payment at scale becomes unaffordable.

Both sides can describe their work as integrity work. Often, they are right. They are seeking the truth. Yet they are also seeking the truth from opposite sides of a financial transaction. The provider wants the record to support the highest accurate payment. The payer wants the record to support the lowest accurate payment. Those statements are not insults. They are incentives.

This is why the administrative labor force has become so large. The revenue cycle management market has been estimated at more than $343 billion in 2024, and it is projected to grow rapidly. The U.S. medical coding market alone was estimated at $21.6 billion in 2025. The American Academy of Professional Coders (AAPC) reports a professional network of more than 200,000 members in coding, billing, auditing, compliance, CDI, and revenue cycle functions, while the American Health Information Management Association (AHIMA) reports more than 60,000 health information professionals worldwide. The Bureau of Labor Statistics counted nearly 195,000 medical records specialists in the United States in 2024. These figures do not capture everyone involved in patient access, billing, collections, payer claims operations, utilization management, legal appeals, compliance, data analytics, or payment integrity. The number of people whose work depends on the complexity of the claim is very large.

That fact matters morally.

It is easy to say that administrative waste should be eliminated. It is harder to say that hundreds of thousands of people, many of whom entered this work in good faith and became experts in a difficult system, should simply lose their livelihoods. Any serious reform has to remember the people inside the machinery. The goal should not be to discard them. It should be to move their expertise toward higher-value work: clinical data quality, patient navigation, compliance, AI supervision, cybersecurity, audit design, appeals that actually involve judgment, and the many places where

---

https://www.kff.org/private-insurance/issue-brief/claims-denials-and-appeals-in-aca-marketplace-plans-in-2024/.

human experience still matters. If reform treats workers as disposable, it will be both politically doomed and ethically thin.

Still, job preservation cannot be the only measure. We do not keep a maze because guides have become good at selling maps. If a portion of our healthcare workforce is spending its life correcting preventable confusion, then the better future is not more confusion. The better future is work that helps patients receive care, helps clinicians document clearly, helps hospitals stay solvent, helps payers pay correctly, and helps the public see where the money is going.

What, then, are the real options?

A National Health System

One proposal is to move to universal health coverage through a national health system, something Americans often summarize, sometimes accurately and sometimes not, as the British model. The *National Health Service* (NHS) in Great Britain is largely funded through general taxation and national insurance contributions, provides comprehensive coverage, and generally does not impose patient cost-sharing for physician and hospital services.[122] That arrangement eliminates many of the most maddening patient-facing bills. There is no ordinary American-style scramble among hospital, physician, facility, and insurer statements when the system is functioning as designed.

The NHS shows that a country can decide that medical care should be financed as a public commitment rather than as a fragmented set of private transactions. That is a powerful lesson. It also shows that simplicity in billing does not abolish scarcity. A national budget has to be set. Services have to be prioritized. Workforce constraints, waiting times, capital investment, and political decisions do not vanish. The labyrinth changes shape. It may become less of a billing maze and more of a budgeting maze.

For an American reader, the most useful lesson from the NHS is not that we can copy it whole. We probably cannot. The history, politics, geography, and institutional structures are different. The British NHS arose in the bleak, post-war years as the people were still reeling from the destruction of World War II. They needed the government to step in and support them. The lesson for the U.S. in the 21st century is that eliminating or greatly reducing patient billing complexity is possible when a country is willing to make financing rules broad, public, and uniform. The patient does not have to be the final claims processor of the household.

---

[122] Sean Boyle, "International Health Care System Profiles: England," Commonwealth Fund, accessed April 26, 2026, https://www.commonwealthfund.org/international-health-policy-center/countries/england.

Multipayer Universal Coverage

A second option is a strengthened version of the *Affordable Care Act* (ACA) model. The ACA did not create a national health service. It left employer coverage largely in place, expanded Medicaid in participating states, created regulated marketplaces, required essential health benefits, prohibited many forms of medical underwriting, and used subsidies to make private coverage more affordable. By early 2025, CMS reported record marketplace enrollment of 24.2 million people, and the national uninsured rate remained near historic lows in 2024.[123] Those are not minor accomplishments.

But the ACA did not remove the American payment labyrinth. It expanded access while leaving multiple payers, plan designs, networks, deductibles, prior authorization rules, claims platforms, and billing practices in place. A person with an ACA marketplace plan may be insured and still not understand an explanation of benefits. A provider may participate with one plan offered by a carrier but not another. A payer may cover a service but deny a particular claim because the documentation, code, modifier, authorization, or site of service is wrong. Coverage is not the same as clarity.

Germany and the Netherlands offer another set of lessons. Germany achieves universal coverage largely through statutory health insurance funds, with most people enrolled in nonprofit sickness funds and a smaller portion covered privately.[124] The Netherlands uses mandatory health insurance through regulated private insurers, with community-rated premiums, risk adjustment, and government involvement in financing.[125] These systems are not single-payer systems in the American shorthand sense. They are multipayer systems, but the rules are more standardized, coverage is universal, and the architecture is built around a national decision that everyone must be covered.

---

[123] Centers for Medicare & Medicaid Services, "Statement from CMS Administrator Chiquita Brooks-LaSure on the Nearly 24 Million People Who Have Chosen Affordable Health Coverage in ACA Marketplace," January 17, 2025, accessed April 26, 2026, https://www.cms.gov/newsroom/press-releases/statement-cms-administrator-chiquita-brooks-lasure-nearly-24-million-people-who-have-chosen; Jennifer Tolbert, Patrick Drake, and Meghana Ammula, "Key Facts about the Uninsured Population," KFF, December 18, 2025, accessed April 26, 2026, https://www.kff.org/uninsured/issue-brief/key-facts-about-the-uninsured-population/.

[124] Michael W. C. C. Schmidt, "International Health Care System Profiles: Germany," Commonwealth Fund, accessed April 26, 2026, https://www.commonwealthfund.org/international-health-policy-center/countries/germany.

[125] Wynand P. M. M. van de Ven and Frederik T. Schut, "International Health Care System Profiles: Netherlands," Commonwealth Fund, accessed April 26, 2026, https://www.commonwealthfund.org/international-health-policy-center/countries/netherlands.

That distinction matters. The United States sometimes acts as if the only choices are a government-run health service or the current patchwork. Other wealthy countries prove otherwise. Universal coverage can coexist with private insurers. Regulated competition can coexist with public financing. Standard benefit packages and risk adjustment can coexist with multiple organizations administering coverage. The hard part is not inventing a model. The hard part is deciding what values the model must serve and then disciplining the system around those values.

Boring Reforms That Would Actually Help

There are, of course, nearer-term reforms that do not require a national redesign. Standardize the most common prior authorization requirements. Require real-time electronic eligibility and benefit answers. Require specific denial reasons written in language that a provider can act on and a patient can understand. Require public reporting of approval rates, denial rates, appeal rates, turnaround times, and reversal rates. Limit prior authorization to services where there is a demonstrable risk of overuse, variation, safety concern, or high cost. Protect continuity of care when patients change plans. Use gold-carding for providers whose authorization requests are almost always approved. Standardize attachments. Retire low-value edits. Make contracts clearer. Make patient responsibility visible before the bill arrives.

These are not glamorous reforms. No one will win an election by promising better attachment standards. Yet much of the pain in medical billing lives in the boring seams. A missing referral number. A nonstandard portal. A payer policy that changes quietly. A claim attachment that disappears into a queue. A patient balance that is generated before the last adjustment posts. The ordinary irritations are not ordinary when multiplied across a national system. They become labor, delay, distrust, and money.

Transparency also has to be more than price lists posted on a website that almost no patient can interpret. A posted hospital charge is not the same thing as a patient's likely responsibility. A negotiated rate is not the same thing as an out-of-pocket estimate. An explanation of benefits is not an explanation if the person reading it still does not know whether to pay. Real transparency should follow the episode from scheduling to claim to payment to patient balance and should tell the patient, in usable language, what happened and what remains uncertain.

These incremental changes would help, but they would not be enough. They would still leave the United States with thousands of payers, countless contracts, multiple payment methodologies, and a clinical record that has to be translated into financial data. That is why the deeper solution has to address the translation itself.

A claim is a statement about what happened to a patient. A payment is a financial answer to that statement. The entire system should be designed so that the most direct path is the truthful path. Today, that is not always the case. Sometimes the fastest path is the code that pays. Sometimes the safest path is the denial that avoids risk.

Sometimes the easiest path is the default documentation copied forward from yesterday. Sometimes the profitable path is the ambiguity that avoids an edit. A healthy payment system should reverse those incentives.

Artificial Intelligence – Real World Benefit

This brings us to the possibility that only recently has begun to look technically plausible: an independent, *artificial intelligence* (AI)-assisted healthcare adjudication process.

I do not mean a payer-owned black box that denies more claims faster. I do not mean a provider-owned coding engine that maximizes payment without restraint. I do not mean a chatbot that guesses at codes from incomplete notes.

I mean something more ambitious and more accountable: a governed, independent translation layer that sits before the a medical care encounter is completed; reviews the clinical record, relevant orders, medication administration records, imaging reports, procedure notes, discharge summaries, payer policies, coding guidelines, contracts, and public payment rules; and then arrives at the correct payment with an explanation for each material code and payment-relevant choice.

The idea would be to move the argument upstream, "moving to the left of the process" in the current medical claim jargon. Instead of the provider submitting a claim, the payer denying it, the provider appealing, the payer reviewing, the patient waiting, and everyone spending money on the delay, the system would attempt to identify the correct payment before submission. The AI would not merely choose a code. It would determine what care was provided, the estimated cost of that care, the reasonable payment for that care, what payer policy applies, and whether human review is needed.

This kind of system would have to be vertical, not generic. A medical coding model cannot be merely a general language model with a stethoscope sticker on it. It would need deep training in medical terminology, payer policies, clinical evidence, documentation standards, healthcare financial information, and the many exceptions that make healthcare payment so frustrating. It has been suggested that domain-specific agents can reason over intent, evaluate different paths, and operate within enterprise-defined policies with human oversight.[126] In healthcare payment, the intent should not be maximizing revenue or minimizing payment. The intent should be an accurate, explainable, auditable payment.

An AI adjudication system that is not explainable will deepen distrust. An AI system that cannot be audited will become another battlefield. An AI system that is controlled by one side will be suspected by the other side. An AI system that

[126] "Systemic Vulnerabilities in US Healthcare: Emerging Solutions," Vlad Panin, Forbes Business Council, 2025.

centralizes too much data without resilient security will create a target too dangerous to tolerate. The Change Healthcare cyberattack in 2024 demonstrated what happens when a deeply embedded administrative intermediary becomes a single point of failure; the *American Hospital Association* (AHA) reported widespread financial and patient-care disruption among hospitals responding to its survey.[127] The lesson is not that clearinghouses and intermediaries are unnecessary. The lesson is that critical administrative infrastructure must be redundant, secure, transparent, and governed as infrastructure.

The cybersecurity literature points in the same direction. Ewoh and Vartiainen's systematic review identified human error, lack of investment, complex network-connected endpoint devices, old legacy systems, and rapid digitalization as major themes explaining healthcare vulnerability to cyberattacks. Their recommended solutions were not merely technical. They emphasized training, awareness, information sharing, secure design, phasing out legacy systems, improved investment, and a sociotechnical framework connecting people, processes, and technology.[128] That is exactly the mindset an AI adjudication layer would require. Healthcare cannot safely automate truth while leaving the surrounding systems brittle.

Such a system would need several non-negotiable features. First, it would need independence. Governance should include providers, payers, patient representatives, regulators, clinicians, coders, security experts, and technologists, but no single group should own the answer. Second, it would need transparency. Each payment-relevant choice should be traceable to record evidence and policy logic. Third, it would need contestability. Humans must be able to challenge the answer, add missing documentation, correct factual errors, and appeal policy interpretations. Fourth, it would need security by design. Multi-factor authentication, segmentation, encryption, immutable audit logs, backup processes, downtime protocols, and independent security testing should not be afterthoughts. Fifth, it would need humility. Low-risk, routine cases might be finalized with minimal review. High-risk, high-dollar, ambiguous, novel, or disputed cases should be routed to human experts.

If this sounds expensive, remember what we are already buying. We are already paying for provider coding, payer editing, CDI, RCM, PI, denial management, appeals, audits, compliance investigations, patient service calls, collection letters, and years of technology built around after-the-fact dispute. The question is not whether we can

---

[127] American Hospital Association, "AHA Survey: Change Healthcare Cyberattack Significantly Disrupts Patient Care, Hospitals' Finances," March 15, 2024, accessed April 26, 2026, https://www.aha.org/2024-03-15-aha-survey-change-healthcare-cyberattack-significantly-disrupts-patient-care-hospitals-finances.

[128] Pius Ewoh and Tero Vartiainen, "Vulnerability to Cyberattacks and Sociotechnical Solutions for Health Care Systems: Systematic Review," Journal of Medical Internet Research 26 (2024): e46904, https://doi.org/10.2196/46904.

afford an accurate pre-claim process. The question is whether we can afford to keep paying for an inaccurate post-claim war.

There are dangers. If AI is trained on past claims data without careful oversight, it may learn the system's bad habits. It may learn that a commonly paid code is correct when it is merely tolerated. It may learn payer-specific denial patterns that reflect administrative convenience rather than clinical truth. It may reproduce inequities embedded in documentation quality, access to specialists, or institutional resources. Rural hospitals and small practices may lack the capital to implement the newest tools unless the system deliberately supports them. Patients may have little visibility into a process that affects their bills unless transparency is required from the beginning.

Those problems are real. They are not reasons to avoid reform. They are reasons to build reform carefully.

A practical path would begin modestly. Start with limited instances where rules are clear, documentation is structured, and payment stakes are meaningful but not catastrophic. Require the AI to produce evidence maps rather than just answers. Compare its recommendations with certified coders, CDI specialists, PI reviewers, and payer adjudication results. Measure not only speed and savings, but accuracy, appeal rates, provider burden, patient confusion, cybersecurity performance, and unintended consequences. Publish enough results to earn trust. Expand only when the evidence says expansion is justified.

Over time, the human roles would change. Coders would become reviewers of complex cases and stewards of data integrity. CDI professionals would focus less on payment maximization and more on real-time clarity in the clinical record. Payers would still need policy, fraud control, medical directors, and appeal processes, but the center of gravity would move from adversarial correction to shared translation.

Patients would not need to know every detail, but they would deserve a clearer answer. Emily's portal should not merely display a balance. It should show, in plain language, what services were recognized, what was paid, why the patient owes anything, and what can be done if the answer appears wrong. The same evidence map that supports the payment could support the patient's explanation. The patient should not have to become a healthcare expert to pay a fair bill.

For What Purpose?

What could be done with the savings? The answer is almost embarrassingly obvious. We could strengthen primary care. We could keep rural hospitals from closing. We could pay nurses and other frontline staff in ways that recognize their value. We could expand behavioral health access. We could reduce premiums, deductibles, or medical debt. We could invest in cybersecurity before the next crisis rather than after it. We could train the workers displaced from low-value administrative tasks into higher-value healthcare roles. We could use the money to make care more humane.

None of this will happen by accident. Every dollar of administrative waste is also someone's revenue. Every inefficiency has a constituency. Every workaround has a defender. Every reform will be accused of threatening autonomy, revenue, jobs, privacy, or patient choice. Some of those accusations will be self-serving. Some will be correct. The task is to separate genuine risk from comfortable inertia.

The history in this book suggests a rule for judging reform: ask whether it makes the truthful path easier than the manipulative path. If a proposal merely shifts leverage from providers to payers, it is not enough. If it merely arms providers with better tools to optimize payment, it is not enough. If it merely gives patients more paperwork in the name of transparency, it is not enough. If it replaces human opacity with algorithmic opacity, it is not enough. A worthy reform should make accurate documentation easier, accurate coding easier, accurate payment faster, denial reasons clearer, appeals rarer, patient responsibility more understandable, and fraud harder.

This is also where the labyrinth metaphor finally earns its keep. Theseus did not escape because the labyrinth became simple. He escaped because he had a thread. The thread did not remove the walls. It gave him a way to move through them without losing himself.

For modern healthcare payment, the thread is honest translation. Clinical truth must become claim truth. Claim truth must become payment truth. Payment truth must become patient truth. Each transformation should preserve meaning rather than distort it.

That is easy to say and hard to build. It will require standardized data, better policies, fewer needless variations, stronger security, wiser use of automation, and humility from people who have learned to win inside the current maze. It will require providers to accept that documentation designed only to increase payment is not integrity. It will require payers to accept that denial without clear explanation is not integrity. It will require vendors to accept that growth built on avoidable confusion is not integrity. It will require regulators to accept that more rules are sometimes less compliance. It will require patients to be treated as participants in the system, not as the last stop for whatever confusion remains.

The Path Behind Us and the Task Before Us

We began with medieval medical care offered under unwritten rules and arrived at a world of claims engines, DRGs, CPTs, HCPCS codes, revenue codes, clearinghouses, payer edits, prior authorizations, denials, appeals, and AI. The journey is not simply a story of decline. The old world was simpler because it asked fewer questions and protected fewer people. The modern world tries to pay fairly across millions of encounters, many forms of illness, many kinds of providers, many kinds of products, and many sources of financing. That ambition is honorable.

But honorable ambition does not excuse unnecessary complexity.

The next chapter of American healthcare payment should not be a war between coders and algorithms, payers and providers, hospitals and patients, public programs and private plans. It should be a disciplined effort to make the record, the claim, the payment, and the bill describe the same reality. If AI helps do that, use it. If universal coverage helps do that, consider it. If regulated multipayer systems offer better guardrails, learn from them. If a small change in a claims standard saves millions of hours, make the change. The point is not to worship any model. The point is to stop mistaking the maze for the mission.

The mission is care. Payment should support it. Billing should explain it. Administration should protect it. Technology should clarify it. And when the bill arrives at the kitchen table, the person holding it should not have to enter the labyrinth alone.

There is a way out.

But we will have to choose the thread.

Chapter 11: Breadcrumbs for the Labyrinth

- The American medical bill is the visible end of a vast translation machine that converts clinical events into codes, edits, contracts, payments, denials, appeals, and patient balances.
- The complexity of the system did not arise from one bad decision. Each layer began as a solution to a real problem, but each also created new incentives and new opportunities for dispute or manipulation.
- Administrative costs in American healthcare are enormous, and even modest reductions in preventable administrative burden could redirect large sums toward care.
- CDI, RCM, PI, coding, claims editing, and denial management employ large numbers of skilled people. Reform should move their expertise toward higher-value work rather than treating them as disposable.
- Universal coverage models such as the NHS can greatly reduce patient-facing billing complexity, but they do not eliminate scarcity or difficult policy choices.
- The ACA expanded coverage and reduced the uninsured rate, but it did not remove the fragmented American payment architecture.
- Germany and the Netherlands show that universal coverage can exist in regulated multipayer systems, but such systems require standardized rules, public discipline, and a national commitment to coverage.
- A promising future solution is an independent, auditable, AI-assisted adjudication translation layer that seeks the accurate payment before the provider and payer begin fighting after the fact.
- AI in medical care payment adjudication must be explainable, contestable, secure by design, and supervised by humans. A black box owned by one side deepens distrust.
- The core test for every reform is whether it makes honest translation easier than strategic ambiguity.

EPILOGUE

It is my hope that your experience of LABYRINTH has been one that matches the original goal set out in the preface: that you now have a better awareness of the challenges facing everyone involved in the American healthcare system.

I believe that key ingredients will be needed to make American healthcare better, and many of those ingredients are dependent on honest, intellectually curious awareness like this book and many others promotes. Some of those ingredients are:

- Empathy – Leaders in government, administrators of provider health systems, for-profit and not-for-profit health plans and other payers, and all of us as individual American citizens have to seek to understand and do what we can to meet the needs of all U.S. residents.
- Pragmatism – Instead of talking ad nauseam about the things that cannot or should not be done, let us as Americans talk about what can be done to improve our healthcare system and then get about to doing it.
- Love – Many of us as Americans adhere to a faith that leads us to love our fellow human beings. All of us have families, friends, and others that call for the same response. While empathy entails understanding so that you can care, love means you care even if you do not fully understand.

It is time to break down the walls of the labyrinth and let in the light.

Breadcrumbs for the Labyrinth: Summary

Chapter 1 showed that payment for medical care was historically personal, status-based, opaque, and shaped by the physician-patient relationship and the long-standing duty to care for the poor.

Chapter 2 showed how ICD, Blue Cross and Blue Shield, employer-based insurance, Hill-Burton, Medicare, and Medicaid created the modern financing framework and the split between facility and professional payment.

Chapter 3 showed that DRGs and prospective payment made inpatient hospital reimbursement more predictable but also made payment highly dependent on documentation and coding.

Chapter 4 showed how CPT, HCPCS, RBRVS, OPPS, APCs, and EAPGs extended coding and payment complexity into physician services, outpatient care, supplies, drugs, and other services.

Chapter 5 showed how CDI, RCM, and PI arose as opposing but often necessary forces in a system where payment depends on the precise translation of the clinical record into claim data.

Chapter 6 showed that claim forms, revenue codes, HCPCS codes, modifiers, edits, and payer contracts can make ordinary care produce many claims and can make strategic ambiguity profitable.

Chapter 7 showed how the complexity built inside claims finally arrives at the patient's kitchen table as bills, EOBs, portal balances, payment plans, collections, and confusion about what is actually owed.

Chapter 8 showed that claims are paid through contracts, not only through codes, and that network status, chargemasters, fee schedules, self-funded employers, TPAs, and price transparency rules all shape what payment means.

Chapter 9 showed how prescription drugs, devices, DME, specialty pharmacies, and physician-administered medications add another maze of codes, formularies, rebates, benefits, and patient costs.

Chapter 10 showed how prior authorization turns coverage rules into a wall around care, sometimes preventing waste and harm, but sometimes delaying treatment, burdening clinicians, confusing patients, and shifting medical risk onto people least able to manage it.

Chapter 11 argues that the purpose of reform should be to make the truthful path easier than the manipulative path, whether the reform comes through universal coverage, regulated multipayer systems, administrative simplification, better prior authorization discipline, or an independent AI-assisted pre-claim truth layer.

The thread out of the labyrinth is honest translation: clinical truth should become claim truth, claim truth should become payment truth, and payment truth should become patient truth.

GLOSSARY

A GUIDE TO THE HEALTHCARE LETTER SALAD

1. AAPC – American Academy of Professional Coders
2. ACA – Affordable Care Act
3. ACDIS – Association of Clinical Documentation Improvement/Integrity Specialists
4. AHA – American Hospital Association
5. AHIMA – American Health Information Management Association
6. AI – Artificial Intelligence
7. AMA – American Medical Association
8. AOC – Add-On Code
9. AP-DRG – All Patient Diagnostic Related Group
10. APC – Ambulatory Payment Classification
11. APR-DRG – All Patient Refined Diagnostic Related Group
12. ASP – Average Sales Price
13. AWP – Average Wholesale Price
14. CAQH – Council for Affordable Quality Healthcare
15. CC – Complicating Condition or complication or comorbidity
16. CDI – Clinical Documentation Improvement/Integrity
17. CFPB – Consumer Financial Protection Bureau
18. CMS – Centers for Medicare and Medicaid Services
19. CPR – Customary, Prevailing, and Reasonable charges
20. CPT – Current Procedural Terminology
21. DME – Durable Medical Equipment
22. DRG – Diagnostic Related Group
23. E & M – Evaluation and Management
24. EAPG – Enhanced Ambulatory Patient Grouping
25. EMR – Electronic Medical Record
26. EOB – Explanation of Benefits
27. ER – Emergency room
28. ERISA – Employee Retirement Income Security Act
29. GDP – Gross Domestic Product
30. HCFA – Health Care Financing Administration
31. HCPCS – Healthcare Common Procedure Coding System

32. HEW – Health, Education, and Welfare – U.S. government department prior to 1980.
33. IBR – Itemized Bill Review
34. ICD – International Classification of Diseases (ICD-10 is the version used in the U.S. in 2026.)
35. IDR – Independent Dispute Resolution
36. IPPS – Inpatient Prospective Payment System
37. ISI – International Statistical Institute
38. MCC – Major Complicating Condition or major complication or major comorbidity
39. MDC – Major Diagnostic Category
40. MRF – Machine-Readable File
41. MS-DRG – Medical (or Medicare) Severity Diagnostic Related Group
42. MUE – Medically Unlikely Edit
43. NCCI – National Correct Coding Initiative
44. NDC – National Drug Code
45. NHS – National Health Service (Britain)
46. NSA – No Surprises Act
47. OPPS – Outpatient Prospective Payment System
48. PA – Prior Authorization
49. PBM – Pharmacy Benefit Manager
50. PI – Payment Integrity
51. POA – Present on Admission
52. PPS – Prospective Payment System
53. PTP – Procedure to Procedure edit
54. RBRVS – Resource-Based Relative Value Scale
55. RCM – Revenue Cycle Management
56. ROC – Return on Capital
57. RUC – Relative Value Scale Update Committee
58. SOI – Severity of Illness
59. TPA – Third-Party Administrator
60. WHO – World Health Organization

ABOUT THE AUTHOR

Timothy J. Garrett lives with his wife Cynthia near Athens, Georgia. He is a physician, a healthcare executive, and an amateur bass player. Visit his website at https://timothyjgarrett.com and connect with him on LinkedIn at www.linkedin.com/in/timothyjgarrett.

www.ingramcontent.com/pod-product-compliance
Lightning Source LLC
LaVergne TN
LVHW022055200926
848481LV00003B/929
* 9 7 9 8 9 9 9 2 0 3 9 0 8 *